International Political Economy

International Political Economy

Understanding Global Disorder

Robert W. Cox

Stephen Gill

Björn Hettne (Editor)

Kees van der Pijl

James N. Rosenau

Yoshikazu Sakamoto

FERNWOOD PUBLISHING
Halifax, Nova Scotia

SAPES SA
Cape Town

UNIVERSITY PRESS LIMITED
Dhaka

ZED BOOKS
London & New Jersey

International Political Economy was first published in 1995 by:

In Canada
Fernwood Books Ltd, PO Box 9409, Station A,
Halifax, Nova Scotia, Canada B3K 5S3

In Southern Africa
(Angola, Botswana, Lesotho, Malawi, Mozambique,
Namibia, South Africa, Swaziland, Zambia, Zimbabwe)
Southern Africa Political Economy Series (SAPES),
50–53 van Riebeeck House, 14 Loop Street,
Cape Town, South Africa

In Bangladesh
The University Press Ltd, Red Crescent Building,
114 Motijheel C/A, PO Box 2611, Dhaka 1000, Bangladesh

In the Rest of the World
Zed Books Ltd, 7 Cynthia Street, London N1 9JF, UK, and
165 First Avenue, Atlantic Highlands, New Jersey 07716, USA

Cover designed by Andrew Corbett
Typeset in Monotype Garamond by Lucy Morton, London SE12
Printed and bound in the United Kingdom
by Biddles Ltd, Guildford and King's Lynn

A catalogue record for this book is available from the British Library
US CIP data is available from the Library of Congress

Canadian Cataloguing in Publication Data
International political economy
Includes bibliographical references and index.
ISBN 1-895686-58-x
1. International economic relations. I. Hettne, Björn, 1939–
HF1359.I58 1995   337   C95-950187-8

CASED EDITION
ISBN 1 85649 295 8 Cased

LIMP EDITION
Canada ISBN 1 895686 58 x Limp
Southern Africa ISBN 0 9584007 5 x Limp
Bangladesh ISBN 984 05 1305 2 Limp
Rest of the World ISBN 1 85649 296 6 Limp

Contents

1 Introduction: The International Political Economy
   of Transformation
   Björn Hettne   1

2 Critical Political Economy
   Robert W. Cox   31

3 Distant Proximities: The Dynamics and Dialectics
   of Globalization
   James N. Rosenau   46

4 Theorizing the Interregnum: The Double Movement
   and Global Politics in the 1990s
   Stephen Gill   65

5 The Second Glorious Revolution: Globalizing Elites
   and Historical Change
   Kees van der Pijl   100

6 Democratization, Social Movements and World Order
   Yoshikazu Sakamoto   129

About the Contributors   144

Index   146

1

Introduction: The International Political Economy of Transformation

Björn Hettne

This book is not so much a general introduction to International Political Economy as a contribution to the study of change and transformation within this relatively new, exciting and growing academic field. This study becomes the more urgent as change, as we now conceive it, implies 'disorder', 'turbulence' or 'chaos', to quote some expressions from the authors of this book. It may be true that 'change' in and of itself is of limited interest (Sörensen, 1994; Vincent, 1983), but what is not to be doubted is that a capacity to handle change and transformation intellectually marks the maturity of a social-science discipline. In the case of International Political Economy this challenge is nothing less than the comprehension of 'global transformation' (Sakamoto, 1994). All the contributions to this book therefore address the problem of how to understand the current era of global uncertainties. But first some general remarks about the specific academic field of International Political Economy are called for.

The Meanings of Political Economy

Political economy is one of the more complex and contested concepts in social science (Staniland, 1985; Caporaso and Levine, 1992). This is consequently also true for the more recent concept of International Political Economy (IPE). According to most introductory textbooks, IPE deals with the way the world economy is organized politically, or how political anarchy can be compatible with international economic cooperation – the non-coincidence of political organization and economic function. More concisely, IPE is the connection between politics and economics in international relations.[1] The crucial issue is how we define this connection.

One important underlying assumption of IPE, which makes it distinct from mainstream international economics, is that no economic system can exist for long without a stabilizing political framework of some sort. Thus the world economy and the international political system cannot be usefully analysed in separation from each other, but must be dealt with within one single theoretical framework, although necessarily informed by several disciplines. Since these disciplines can in themselves be understood as the result of a fragmentation of classical political economy, the study of IPE can also be seen as a contribution to a reconstituted social science, primarily aimed at overcoming the artificial distinctions between economic-political, on the one hand, and domestic-international, on the other.

Political economy is a long-established but at the same time rather elusive concept. While some would say that it represents the very core of social science, others may fear that the holism it implies spells the end of what we mean by the modern social sciences. This is because it seems to contradict scientific achievements presumed to have been gained through academic specialization; for instance, the study of what is understood as 'economic man', not to speak of an equally strange creature called 'political man'.

Political economy is compatible with widely differing ideological and theoretical perspectives or paradigms, which further adds to its elusiveness. Although political economy was always an ideological battlefield, there is a consensus about what conventionally constitutes, or at least has in the past constituted, the fundamental concern of political economy, namely the interaction of state and market, or, in different terms, politics and economics:

> Without both state and market there would be no political economy. In the absence of the state, the price mechanism and market forces would determine the outcome of economic activities; this would be the pure

world of the economist. In the absence of the market, the state or its equivalent would allocate economic resources; this would be the pure world of the political scientist. (Gilpin, 1987: 8)

There are, however, many approaches to choose from:

Each approach may define what constitutes the 'political' and the 'economic', and their integration into a particular 'political economy', in different ways. (Gill and Law, 1988: 15)

Essentially, the two logics – of the state and of the market – are seen as incompatible:

The logic of the market is to locate economic activities where they are most productive and profitable; the logic of the state is to capture and control the process of economic growth and capital accumulation. (Gilpin, 1987: 11, quoting Heilbroner, 1985: 94–5)

The easy way is to build a discipline upon each of these logics. Hence we have political science and economics. The hard part is to combine them. However, transcending or synthesizing attempts are also being made:

Many examples of modern Political Economy transcend the arbitrary distinction between the political and the economic. (Jones, 1988: 1)

What I am suggesting here is a way to synthesize politics and economics by means of structural analysis of the effects of states – or more properly of any kind of political authority – on markets and, conversely, of market forces on states. (Strange, 1988: 13–14)

There are also different views on the relative importance of the state vis-à-vis the market. Neither should be seen as primary; their relationship is interactive and dialectical, as shown in Karl Polanyi's pioneering contribution to this field (Polanyi, 1957). For instance, Robert Cox mentions Karl Polanyi together with Antonio Gramsci and Fernand Braudel as sources of inspiration so far as the understanding of structural change is concerned. Polanyi has, furthermore, been viewed as the 'most influential forerunner of world-system analysis' (Ágh, 1990), and many of the current research questions in IPE formed part of his conceptual and theoretical

framework. The era to which he gave the name the 'Great Transformation' thus largely coincided with the rise and decline of British
hegemony. The current debate is, rather, about the implications of
the decline of US hegemony.

In this introduction I will relate the contemporary discussion on
change in the international system to Polanyi's now fifty-year-old
magnum opus *The Great Transformation* (originally published in 1944),
for the reason that the contributors to this volume favour an
approach to the study of change in the global political economy
that is exemplified by, if not identified with, Polanyi's work.

Outside IPE, Polanyi is better-known for a number of other
important conceptual innovations to further what he called a 'substantive', in contradistinction to 'formal', understanding of economic
reality. It should be emphasized, however, that his concepts form
a framework within which societal transformation can be fruitfully
analysed. A comparison can be made with Gramsci, who also
provided us with a set of useful concepts (hegemony, civil society,
historic bloc) which were used contextually rather than in a transhistorical manner.

The concept of *market*, for instance, has according to Polanyi
two meanings: one concrete, namely the marketplace, another
abstract, referring to the market system. Marketplaces are a more
or less universal phenomenon, as we can learn from history and
anthropology. They all operate in accordance with the same basic
logic, regardless of how the society at large has chosen to institutionalize economic life. The prices of those goods that are ex-
changed on the market fluctuate according to supply and demand
conditions, and determine the 'profits' of different commodities in
the short run and resource allocation between the production of
different commodities ('investment') in the long run.

Historically, marketplaces were atypical forms of economic
exchange, accountable to and restricted by political and social
controls. The complete domination of societies by the market
principle, implying that land, capital and labour have also been
commodified, is a recent phenomenon. Two other mechanisms of
economic integration have existed historically: *reciprocity* and *redistribution*. The former refers to the socially embedded forms of

exchange in small-scale symmetrical communities, the latter to politically determined distribution in stratified societies marked by a centre–periphery structure. Both modes of distribution were undermined by the growth of market exchange.

However, as the market principle penetrated all spheres of human activity, thereby eroding social structures, redistribution had to be reinvented in order to provide people with the necessary social protection. Polanyi called this type of reaction on the part of society the second part of a 'double movement', the first part being the expansion and deepening of market exchange. This was the origin of the modern welfare state, as well as of other types of interventionist economy. Thus, modern industrial societies were typically distinguished by a market–redistribution mix. Depending on the nature of this mix we called some 'capitalist' and others 'socialist'. In neither system does reciprocity play a role in economic transactions outside the family and kinship groups. After the present phase of neo-liberal hegemony and social marginalization, reciprocity – or what in other theoretical frameworks is called 'community' or 'civil society' – is bound to become more important again, simply as a mode of survival when the protective redistributive political structures break up (Hettne, 1990).

Contemporary scholars in the field of IPE rarely refer to Polanyi as a pioneer. The contributors to this book are exceptions in this regard. The methodology of Polanyi, and above all the historical (in contrast to the historicist) approach, should inspire future work in the field of IPE. The idea of the double movement involves more than redistributive responses. As some contributors to this book emphasize, social movements can also be seen as protective measures in an era of extreme market dominance.

Thus, the inclusion of civil society together with a strong historical dimension constitute important contributions by Polanyi to IPE. In spite of its ambition to integrate the 'political' and the 'economic', current IPE gives only a partial view of society, particularly of societal change. We can perhaps define a New International Political Economy as attempts to go beyond the state–market contradiction, without necessarily implying that such an academic innovation yet exists in a distinct and homogeneous form

(Murphy and Tooze, 1991). It should be stressed that these are still no more than attempts, probably because to achieve the break-through would necessitate the construction of a broader theoretical foundation, a *historical social science*. By this I mean an integrated study of society as sequential historical structures, each essentially different from what went before.

This emerging body of thought ought to be informed by classical political economy, which in some respects was more complex and richer in content than modern political economy, not to speak of what is known as 'the new political economy'. The reason for this is that modern political economy is usually seen as a marriage between political science and economics, which of course did not exist as specialized disciplines when classical political economy was founded. IPE, for its part, is definitely something more than a marriage between international economics and world politics. As Robert Cox emphasizes in his contribution to this volume, political economy is concerned with structures within which political *and* economic activities take place. To distinguish the political from the economic is usually a very artificial exercise. This is also the case with efforts to create a pure political economy. More recently, efforts have instead been made to conceptualize a 'global political economy' (Gill and Law, 1988; Peterson and Runyan, 1993). Since we are dealing with a new and only partially known structure, this conceptualization is necessarily tentative. We can assume, however, that there will be a very different role for the state in this post-Westphalian complex, multi-level world (Cox, 1993).

IPE in the Past

Political economy is hard to distinguish from underlying competing ideologies about the organization of economic life. When it first appeared as a comprehensive doctrine, political economy argued in favour of a market-oriented economy, liberated from the statist practice which marked the seventeenth and eighteenth centuries and which was later given the label 'mercantilism'. The historical context of this fundamental political conflict and the doctrine to which it gave birth was the early process of state formation. Mercantilism can thus best be understood as the political economy of state-building.

The essence of 'liberalism' (albeit that the label was applied only in retrospect) is a critique not only of autocratic government but of the state as such. Market solutions to the problem of resource allocation are, according to the liberal view, seen as inherently 'natural'; and the evolution, as well as the emerging hegemony, of the market stands out as the essence of development. However, the liberal tradition, particularly in the case of major figures like Adam Smith, David Ricardo and John Stuart Mill, contains principally important scientific enquiries going beyond the immediate political issues of the day. I am referring to problems such as the sources of economic value and the dynamics of economic development.

Each tradition of political economy in fact contains elements which transcend the particular contexts in which they took shape, thereby assuming a more general significance. The second tradition relates to the mercantilist practice, but in a new and qualitatively different historical context: *the modernization imperative*, that is, the need for modern states to catch up with more advanced industrial countries in order to avoid being eaten by them. This particular logic forms part of the European state system. The classic conflict was the one between Great Britain and Germany: 'cosmopolitical political economy' versus 'national political economy'. These labels were used by F. List, the founder of national political economy, which has also been labelled *mercantilist* or *realist* political economy. 'Mercantilism' is here used in a different and broader sense from when the concept first appeared. I have suggested that it can be defined as 'the pursuit of stateness' (Hettne, 1993a and 1993b). This implies interstate conflicts, particularly between countries with a strong position in the world economy and those who try to catch up. In his contribution to this book (Chapter 5), Kees van der Pijl speaks of a Hobbesian Counterpoint of contender states to the dominant Lockeian heartland.

The third tradition, Marxism, took shape as a 'Critique of Political Economy', that is, as a reaction against the liberal tradition, and can only be understood in that context. This is because Marx did his economic analysis largely within a Ricardian framework (which he also tried to transcend). Its persistence can to some extent be explained by the ultimate demise of classical political economy, symbolized in the change of label from political economy to economics. The 'economic' was unlinked from the 'political' and analysed as a self-regulating system with a logic of its own. 'Man' became 'economic man'.

All theory ultimately has to adapt to changes in the real world. The transnationalization of economic life is one such change. This change, underlying the whole process of globalization, has made many assumptions of political economy irrelevant. Political economy was consequently reborn as IPE. In the IPE context, the perspectives associated with the three historical traditions outlined above are instead related to the dynamics of a transnationalized world economy and its possible political frameworks. A brief description with a special focus on change and transformation will be given here.

Liberal International Political Economy is still the mainstream, but compared to the others it has a less distinct identity, since a liberal international economy is in principle no different from a liberal national economy. The liberal vision is that of a borderless world, at least as far as economic activities are concerned. The difference is quantitative, a matter of the size of the market. Most liberals were free traders, and the term 'liberalism' was in fact used by their opponents as a rather pejorative term, suggesting lack of (state) control and (therefore) irresponsibility (Tooze, 1988: 12). The recent breakdown of the socialist subsystem seemed to confirm the liberal principle: the 'unnatural' sooner or later gives in to the 'natural'. Any attempt to isolate oneself from market forces is thus a sentence to stagnation. The optimum size of an economy (and therefore the ultimate form) is the world market. All other arrangements, for instance regional trade arrangements, are only second best, but acceptable to the extent that they are stepping stones rather than stumbling blocks to the world market. In a fundamentalist liberal perspective, change is the transformation of an incomplete world economy still regulated by political actors into a fully integrated and self-regulating world economy. According to a more pragmatic view, a functioning world economy would require transnational 'regimes' as stabilizers in various sectors (Krasner, 1982).

Marxist International Political Economy does not really start with Marx, who essentially analysed capitalism as a closed system which, rightly or wrongly, came to be taken by many of his followers to coincide with the national economy (Brown, 1988). Its concern with the dynamics of global capitalism came later, more precisely in the era of 'imperialism', which in this ideological perspective meant above all inter-capitalist rivalry paving the way for the First World War. After the Russian Revolution and the rise of a state-sanctioned Marxist orthodoxy, less of theoretical interest happened as far as IPE is concerned, until the rise of structuralist, dependency and world-system theories in the 1960s and the 1970s. This 'neo-Marxist' tradition contradicted the classic Marxist view in crucial respects (Blomström and Hettne, 1984). Particularly in the form of world-system theory, this approach must be said to lack the power to explain how the world system with its centre–periphery structure may as such be transformed. This has been pointed out by more classical Marxism, which for its part has been criticized for being too deterministic. Another unorthodox tradition, with perhaps unexpected relevance for International Relations and IPE theory, emerged with the rediscovery of Gramsci and the so-called 'critical school' (Gill, 1993). Its closeness to the historical reality it is trying to explain makes it more relevant also when it comes to understanding change.

Realist International Political Economy focuses in particular on the nation-state system and the role of international political relations in the organization of the world economy. In the modern context, 'realist' usually refers to the 'neo-realist' tradition, which acknowledges other actors apart from states, and other sources of power apart from military strength. The eclectic and pragmatic approach of the Realist School makes it the dynamic core in the current development of IPE, but also the vaguest of the three traditions (Jones, 1988: 163). It is also ambiguous in the way it deals with change. Changes in the state system are related to the power capabilities of states, but there is no notion of transition from Westphalian to post-Westphalian. The stress is more upon continuity than on transformation. However, as Cox has pointed out, classical realism (in contrast to neo-realism) can, due to its disregard for public ritual, serve the purpose of critical theory as well. In his words, 'Machiavelli's *Prince* appears to be addressed to the powerful, to the *palazzo*. In effect, his work instructs the outsiders in the mechanisms of power, it enlightens the *piazza*'. (Cox, 1991: 18).

Before we enter the current debate, it should be noted that the three intellectual traditions interact, which is the reason why they can be said to form part of a single field. The liberal insistence on the need to maintain a reasonable efficiency through exposure to competition is today universally acknowledged. But this will not for long imply a complete neglect of the 'national interest'. At the same time, the main body of IPE shows an increasing openness to Marxist and other heterodox ideas, as can be seen in the emergence and wide acceptance of the 'critical school' (Ashley, 1984; Cox, for instance in this volume). It seems as if turbulence in world politics and disorder in international relations – to a larger degree than stability – calls for eclecticism and methodological rethinking. Neither of the classical traditions really explains why changes occur (Staniland, 1985), vacillating as they do between economism and politicism. Furthermore, they largely neglect the problem of development in the South, which further underlines their partial and static orientation (Hettne, 1995).

IPE and Transformation

Judging from the current debate in IPE and International Relations theory, we live in a period of 'transformation' or 'transition'. In historical studies of transition from one system to another, we have the record – that is, both the starting points and the end points are known to us. In studies of contemporary 'transitions' or processes of transformation, we don't know the end points. Since 'transition' can only refer to a completed process (when one social order has been replaced with a different one), or the general intention behind the process (the striving for socialism or market society), I shall instead use the concept of transformation; more specifically, I will do this in the Polanyi tradition, in which modern society is understood both as a result of market expansion ('the first movement') and as the self-protection of society against the disruptive and destabilizing effects of the market ('the second movement').

The qualitative change in the economic and social structure of European society that Polanyi called the Great Transformation was ultimately caused by the market system and the movement – under British hegemony, the Gold Standard, and the Balance of Power era (the Long Peace) – towards complete dominance of this system over alternative principles of economic organization, that is, reciprocity and redistribution as discussed earlier. The redistributive responses to social turbulence, such as the welfare state, the fascist state and the communist state, were not compatible and therefore did not constitute a viable world order, nor a security order comparable to the Long Peace. The result was a second world war; and at this point Polanyi's analysis ends with a big question mark regarding the postwar social order. Rather than a new hegemonic order (the most likely candidate as hegemon being the USA), facilitating a continued growth of market forces, he preferred a regionalized world order, the 'order' being based on the principle of long-term planning (Polanyi, 1945).

As market exchange can only be amoral, or morally neutral, it is for the political regime to deal with the unintended and/or unwanted consequences of the way in which an unregulated market operates. Thus, society also changes in accordance with the double movement, which means that the economy tends to be re-embedded in society. Paradoxically, even the process of becoming disembedded presupposes a strong and consciously active state. The market cannot liberate itself; neither can it organize society! It reflects, rather, the character of the society and its particular social order, or lack of social order.

To the followers of the Polanyi tradition, among which I and other contributors to this volume count ourselves, the political, redistributive logic (or the logic of the state) stands out as less destructive than the anarchistic logic of the market itself (Polanyi–Levitt, 1990; Mendell and Salée, 1991). Apart from the redistributive response, which Polanyi perhaps overemphasized, the potential of civil society (or, in more Polanyian terms, the principle of reciprocity) is now increasingly discussed as a means for the powerless and the poor. The fundamental problem in a process of transformation is to understand the substantive character of market exchange, and what possible substitutes there are in the institutionalization of economic life, in the future as well as in the past (Polanyi, 1957).

The supporting evidence for an ongoing transformation is the frequency with which the prefixes 'post-' and 'neo-' are added to concepts which describe a particular social order. We are now 'post-' something, whether post-Keynesian, post-Fordist, 'post-modern', 'post-hegemonic', 'post-Westphalian', 'post-international', or 'post-Columbian'; and we need a 'neo-' something, whether 'neo-realism', 'neo-liberal institutionalism', 'neo-Marxism', 'neo-mercantilism', 'neo-structuralism', or 'neo-idealism', in order to understand what is going on and where we are heading.[2]

Let me consider one of these conceptualizations that seems quite useful, namely 'post-Westphalian'. First, what do we mean by 'Westphalian'? By use of this term, Cox (personal communication) refers to the concept of an interstate system derived from the principles that scholars have attributed to the peace of Westphalia that concluded the Thirty Years' War in 1648: the sovereign independence of states; each state being motivated in its international behaviour by a consistent national interest; the interstate system regulated by a balance of power among the principal powers. There is necessarily a particular political rationality underlying this behaviour. The Westphalian rationality takes a particular state as the given guarantee for security as well as welfare. What is outside the state borders is chaos and anarchy. The disorder and turbulence people experience today comes with the realization that this guarantee can no longer be taken for granted. The post-Westphalian logic implies that the nation-state has lost much of its usefulness and that solutions to the problems of security and welfare must, therefore, be found in transnational structures, global or regional.

What images of the current transformation and implications for the future are conveyed by post-Westphalian and other 'post-' concepts? We are saying farewell to a world made up of sovereign states divided into two hostile but stable blocs which shared competitively in a process of modernization, structured by a hegemonic order, the content of which was marked by American civilization. And what methodological conclusions can we draw? In order to understand the emerging world, we must be less state-centric; we have to understand global dynamics in the context of pluralism; 'low politics' will become 'high politics', Western civilization will be increasingly challenged, and risks as well as possibilities will increase.

As a holistic and interdisciplinary social-science approach, IPE raises specific problems. The combination of a large number of different types of variable, the complex interrelationship between 'levels' of society, the emphasis on qualitative factors, and an interest in structural change, all make the verification or falsification of theoretical propositions particularly difficult. The situation is made even more complex by the fact that we only have one international political economy at a time.

One would assume that the contending theories in IPE provide partial insights into the basic research problem: structural changes in the international political economy. In this problem orientation, IPE comes close to what Skocpol (1984) discusses as 'historical sociology'; and at least two of her examples of leaders in this field, Polanyi and Wallerstein, are also central to the IPE field. This underlines the difficulties involved in setting scientific boundaries.

'Historical sociology' is not an adequate term. It should be noted that Skocpol (1984: 4) also seems to have something more general than sociology in mind:

> In my view historical sociology is better understood as a continuing ever-renewed tradition of research devoted to understanding the nature and effects of large-scale structures and fundamental processes of change.

Sociology adds important dimensions to the understanding of world society (Robertson, 1992; Scholte, 1993; Shaw, 1994), but like conventional IPE it is nevertheless insufficiently holistic. *Historical social science* would, as suggested above, come closer to an appropriate designation. This is also the term chosen by Wallerstein for the project of renewing social science (Wallerstein, 1991); but of course the mere invention of a term does not solve our problem. Rather, the various disciplines must simultaneously work towards the goal of a holistic understanding of global change. I have elsewhere suggested that development theory has in its own way served the purpose of preparing for such a project (Hettne, 1995).

The emphasis on history is essential, however. IPE deals also with concrete historical structures: for instance, the two hegemonic global structures in the nineteenth and twentieth centuries. I earlier referred to the role of British hegemony in the Polanyian interpretation of the first Great Transformation. The idea of hegemony in fact appears in several traditions, but with different meanings. A brief overview, indicating the differences in approach, will have to suffice here.

The *Theory of Hegemonic Stability*, pioneered by Kindleberger (1973), elaborated by Gilpin (1981), and succinctly formulated by Keohane (1980), asserts that an open world economy requires a dominant global power for its smooth functioning. Since the issue concerns the essential nature of the postwar order, it would be unrealistic to expect a consensus on how to interpret it. The interpretations vary from neo-realist to neo-Marxist and Gramscian. These schools accept the importance of hegemony for the maintenance of a liberal world economy, while the liberal (or 'neo-liberal institutionalist') position (Keohane, 1984, 1989), as well as that of most international economists, is that interdependence would be possible in a post-hegemonic world through the self-interest of the trading states (the invisible hand applied to international economics).

For Robert Cox (1983, 1991, and Chapter 2 of this volume), using hegemony in the Gramscian sense of a structure of values and understandings, the ideological dimension of hegemonic power stands out as more important than the military and economic dimensions. The significance of hegemony is that it is unquestioned, which implies that the very fact that US hegemony is called into question already means a loss in hegemonic power. A hegemony is a consensual order which can decline as a consequence of a legitimacy deficit, even if the coercive power resources as such should remain intact. Reduction in military capability is compatible with maintenance of a hegemonic position: to the extent that the leadership role of the hegemon continues to be accepted, hegemony on the level of the world order can thus be described as a form of world governance, that is, a set of rules backed by the authority (and credibility) of the hegemon. Hegemony can be seen as a special kind of power, based on different but mutually supportive dimensions, fulfilling certain functions (the providing of international collective goods) in a larger system which lacks formal authority structure, and consequently is more or less voluntarily accepted by other actors.

The analysis of hegemonic structures should, however, be seen as forming part of a larger issue: what constitutes a world order. It is a basic premiss for all political economists that a market, in order to function, presupposes some kind of *order*, a concept which contains both coercive and consensual dimensions. Recent debate has focused on the role of hegemonic stability and, to the extent that this role is considered essential for the functioning of the international economy, the implications of hegemonic decline.[3]

Increased rivalry and conflict among capitalist countries also has a bearing on the problem of succession, that is, the question of the potential new hegemon. In a historical (and realist) perspective this problem has been resolved through wars (Modelski, 1978; Gilpin, 1981; Kennedy, 1987). Limited wars may still serve the purpose of asserting or denying hegemonic claims, particularly in the case of regional great powers. However, the emerging battleground is economic competition, possibly between emerging trade blocs. Based on its multidimensional hegemonic power, the USA has so far provided the rules, summed up in the Bretton Woods system, which has constituted the framework for economic interdependence over the last couple of decades. Consequently, a decline in US hegemonic power seems to imply a world governance crisis: for instance, in the form of nationalist and protectionist policies, challenging the existing rules of the game and making the world economy more fragmented and less stable. There is one debate on the theory of hegemonic stability as such, and another that deals with the issue as to whether a case for US decline really can be made. Both propositions have been challenged, and sometimes the two debates are mixed up in a confusing way.[4] Perhaps the issue has now been overtaken by real events. It is true that in absolute and even relative terms the USA is by far the most powerful state; but, as discussed above, hegemonic power is a very special kind of power. To the extent that the USA takes upon itself the role of hegemon, it will differ from the Cold War period when hegemony was exercised in a tense bipolar context and containment of communism was a major goal. What seems clear is that the will to exercise hegemonic power is markedly reduced even if the capacity has remained intact, which is under dispute.[5]

This raises a number of important research questions, which a future-oriented IPE has to address. Can we expect a new hegemonic power to emerge? The two main candidates are Japan and the New Europe. Neither is very self-assertive at the moment, troubled as they are by difficult adaptations and internal divisions.

The '1992 project' in Europe was a social myth, skilfully created by Jacques Delors, in order to facilitate the development of European competitiveness and leverage on world affairs. It was based on the market utopia, and neglected other relevant issues – for instance, 'domestic' legitimacy and a capacity to solve regional crises. The Maastricht Treaty was meant to provide the means to handle these issues. The continuous democratic deficit, the very high level of unemployment, the failure to find a common solution to monetary turbulence, and the unsuccessful attempts to solve the Balkan crisis show how far Europe still has to go and even raise doubts about its capacity to ever get there.

And what about Japan: will it remain number two in a Pax Americana or take a more independent global role? The latter option, more likely in a longer perspective, would mean the accumulation of military strength and a break with the introverted Japanese world-view. Alternatively, Japan will again become a regional hegemon. The pressure on Japan to decide which is the way forward is increasing due to the regionalist trend in the world economy.

IPE and the Future

IPE, like social science as a whole, must also be able to tell us something useful about the future. As suggested by Rosenau in his contribution to this volume (Chapter 3): 'A more theoretically-conscious policy-making community might have more thoroughly framed the policies needed to foster a new world order and cope with the new challenges it poses.' In future-oriented IPE the crucial question is the following: what will a post-Westphalian and post-hegemonic world order look like? Of course there is no consensus on this issue since the very notion of hegemonic stability is contested. Is it based on material power and dominance, institutions, or an intersubjective moral order? One way of classifying several possible post-hegemonic scenarios currently being discussed in the IPE literature is to identify them on a continuum between two contrasting models of world order: global interdependence and a fragmented world.

One scenario, which may be called *interdependence based on multilateralism*, has a number of variants, but in all of them globalization will continue to run its course. It could, for instance, be a neo-liberal world of trading and mutually dependent nations that have all successfully found a niche in the structure of world commerce (Rosecrance, 1986).

A related scenario is the formation of *international regimes* (systems of management) in specific realms (trade, oceans, finance, energy) where nations comply with established norms without hegemonic pressure. Multilateral institutions would here furnish the confidence previously provided by the hegemon (Keohane 1984, 1989). Such more selective 'post-hegemonic' cooperation also relies on the self-interest of nation-states forming part of an open world economy on which they also depend for their security and welfare. For any participant the costs of breaking the rules of a specific regime is thus higher than complying with them. Keohane, the best-known proponent of this view, calls it 'neoliberal institutionalism'.

International regimes do not cover all forms of international behaviour and therefore imply more fragmentation than the pure multilateral model.

A third scenario, more to the centre of the continuum but nevertheless assuming an open world economy, is some kind of tripartite division of the world into so-called 'megamarkets': North America (now organized in NAFTA), Europe (partly organized in the EU), and Pacific Asia (albeit still lacking a formal organization). The *trilateralist scenario*, in which the three capitalist centres, the USA, Western Europe and Japan, take a shared hegemonic responsibility, also assumes a more or less open world economy (Gill, 1990). Here international economic institutions and multinational corporations, rather than nation-state actors, take predominance.

A more conflictual and consequently more deeply fragmented variant is that of a world economy consisting of competing trading blocs, sometimes called the *Triad*. Depending on the gravity of conflict, this polarization may even indicate a transition to a more closed, regionalized world economy.

A fifth scenario is thus a more territorial type of fragmentation: a form of *regionalization* of the world into more or less self-contained blocs with stable internal structures and interregional relations. The region as such here emerges as an actor, and one may therefore speak of 'extended nationalism'.

The fragmentation may – although this is not very likely in the present era of globalization – go even further towards economic nationalism and *protectionism*: a regression to more classical 'mercantilism'. This would imply a breakdown of the system of interdependence, and a dramatic increase in the level of disorder and decrease in the level of welfare in most regions.

One emerging form of regionalization is the 'new regionalism', defined as a multidimensional process of regional integration which includes economic, political, social and cultural aspects (Hettne and Inotai, 1994). The concept clearly goes far beyond the 'common market' idea, that is, the interlinking of several previously more or less secluded national markets into one functional economic unit. Rather, the political ambition of creating territorial identity and regional coherence is the primary neo-regionalist motive. In order to consolidate the structure of interdependence, however, a certain amount of interventionism would be needed: for instance, in the form of an organized transfer of resources from rich to poor countries. Compared to such 'neo-Keynesianism', arguing for an expansionary economic policy within the framework of a larger but more extroverted region, 'neo-mercantilism' is a more introverted form of the 'new regionalism', aiming at a 'region-state' and 'extended nationalism'.

A great deal of empirical research is needed to be able to assess the realism of the various scenarios, which furthermore can be combined in different ways. The crucial issue seems to be the balance between functional and territorial principles: the universal economic interdependence between increasingly non-territorial economic actors in a completely globalized world versus neo-mercantilist politicization and regionalization of the world economy (Hettne, 1993a and 1993b; Hettne and Inotai, 1994). The future world order will be shaped by the way the contradiction between these two principles is resolved.

Let us now return to Polanyi to see whether his analysis of the Great Transformation has something to tell us about the situation of today. Basic insights and ideas in social science remain relevant, even if they have to be adapted to new situations. To my mind the concept of a 'regionalized world order' is just such an idea, originally developed by Polanyi in an article in 1945 but rarely referred to in the political economy literature. This was just after the conclusion of a great war, when the eventual shape of the new world order was an open question, a situation structurally similar to the one we are currently living through after the Cold War. The USA was then preparing itself for its role as the guardian of the still-to-be-born Bretton Woods system. Polanyi warned against the inherent instability of a liberal world order based on the market and hegemonic powers, and argued in favour of a regional world order with some element of planning which he considered to be a more stable system than the various universalisms criticized in the article. One of them, the universalized market utopia, can be compared to what today is discussed as 'globalization', particularly economic globalization.

If globalization is interpreted primarily as 'economic', and regionalization primarily as 'political', then their relationship is of course a core issue in IPE. Polanyi's crucial question of how to build 'freedom in a complex society' is more urgent and more difficult than ever. Contrary to what Polanyi expected (or at least hoped for), another hegemonic order was established after the war. Pax Americana was, like Pax Britannica that went before it, based on a security order, namely the Cold War system, and an economic order, namely the Bretton Woods system. The economic order permitted a long 'golden age' period of stable growth in the world economy. The system was based upon a compromise between international free trade and domestic regulation based on Keynesianism – what Ruggie has termed the compromise of 'embedded liberalism' (Ruggie, 1983). Those pillars are now gone. US hegemony is declining, the Bretton Woods system has collapsed, and the Cold War system has yet to be replaced by a viable security order. We are in a new turbulent period of disorder, waiting for the second 'double movement' of regulation and social protection, further complicated by the issue of ecological protection. The challenges are enormous.

Regional cooperation as such is not a new idea, but it is now possible to see the early signs of the 'new regionalism' throughout the world. What, then, is the connection between the two ideas; the 'new regionalism' and the double movement? Previously, the self-protection of society was carried out mainly by the state, on the level of the nation-state. This is no longer possible (for small and weak states it never was); and it is my contention that the 'new regionalism' should be seen as a manifestation of the second movement, the self-protection of society, on the level of the region, as a social reaction against the global market expansion which took place in the 1980s and still is the predominant trend today, albeit increasingly questioned.

In terms of Polanyi's framework, there could also be a new rise of reciprocal structures in the form of localism – local structures of self-help and solidarity – as supplements to redistributive structures in the form of regionalism. This would certainly involve a complex system of interacting levels, with a stronger role for supranational and subnational levels, and a diminished role for the nation-state level (post-Westphalianism). This may, again following Polanyi, prevent fascism (linked to a Westphalian mentality) and create 'freedom in a complex society' as the positive alternative to war among civilizations or urban jungles of criminal mafias, so vividly and usually correctly described in neo-conservative writings, but without a hint of what should be done.

The Contributions to this Volume

Without wanting to force the authors of this book into a particular theoretical school, it can be said that they share a normative and future-oriented approach, that they agree on the need for ontological self-consciousness, and that all hold the view that the key to understanding the future lies in history rather than in ahistorical abstractions. In this respect they are all sympathetic to a Polanyian approach. The authors have all been associated with a research programme committed to understanding and reinterpreting the international political economy, namely the MUNS programme (Multilateralism and the United Nations System) sponsored by the United Nations University. Most of the contributors participated in a lecture day in the summer of 1993 at the University of Oslo devoted to new trends in International Political Economy.

The basic concern of the MUNS programme is to analyse the relationship between the changing structure of the world order and the process of international organization. Furthermore, the project entertains the idea of a New Multilateralism, wider in scope than the conventional concept that implies little more than politics of the UN General Assembly and/or equal access to the global trade regime. The broader concept, in contrast, includes relations between actors in civil society; the implications of the biosphere conceived as an active societal force for the human condition and for political behaviour; and, above all, the possibility for global cultural pluralism, or what the research programme refers to as the coexistence of different value systems, a 'supra-intersubjectivity' that would reconcile culturally distinct intersubjectivities (Cox, 1993: 265).

Robert Cox, the intellectual father of the MUNS programme as well as of the Gramscian school in IPE, opens this volume with the assertion that the principal task for IPE today is to construct a mental framework adequate to comprehend the profound and inter-acting structural changes that are going on, rendering the 'West-phalian system' increasingly obsolete. The system is being replaced by a multilevel order, and structures of political authority are form-ing above and below the level of states: macro- and micro-regions, as well as social movements at the base of society. In order to grasp these complex changes theory is essential, and theory can be of two kinds: either its aim is to maintain the existing social order (problem-solving theory) or to change it (critical theory). Cox, in common with the other authors in this volume, belongs to the second cat-egory. In fact political economy, in contrast to political science and economics, which deal with actors rather than structures, is critical theory. Structures, however, must be dealt with diachronically. Historical structures contain both coherence and elements of contra-diction, and transformation should be studied as it derives from these points of conflict. And in this Polanyi showed the way.

James Rosenau, in a similar vein, stresses the need for theory, a theoretical imperative even, in order to grasp what in a major work (Rosenau, 1990) he has called 'Turbulence in World Politics'. To quote a passage from this book:

> Of course it is conceivable that all the chaos does reflect randomness. Such a conclusion, however, should be based on more than impres-sions. At the very least, it is a conclusion that ought not to be reached without first exploring the possibility that appearances are deceiving, that all the disorder we observe is, in fact ordered, if not orderly.

In his chapter, Rosenau further explores the tension between the dynamics of globalization and those pressing in the opposite direc-tion toward fragmentation, localization and individualization. These processes are causally linked; that is, we are dealing with a specific phenomenon, that of 'fragmegration' (a concept combining frag-mentation and integration). This idea is quite compatible with Polanyi's 'double movement' in its dialectical combination of disintegrative and integrative forces.

Stephen Gill, here as in earlier works (1990, 1993), seeks inspiration in Antonio Gramsci's writings in analysing contradictions between globalizing and territorially based social forces. The quotation from Gramsci with which Gill opens the chapter might have provided a motto for this book: 'The old is dying, the new is being born, and in the interregnum there are many morbid symptoms.' Gill, however, sees the present chaos as 'organized chaos', since it corresponds to the interest of class forces pressing for a deregulated disciplinary order, as expressed in neo-liberal orthodoxy. Therefore the world order itself is by definition a turbulent order, and change means not the search for order but the replacement of one order by another. Gill here uses the metaphor of the 'double movement' with reference to sociopolitical forces asserting democratic control over capital. Counterhegemonic politics must, however, be redefined away from totalizing visions, whether fundamentalist or economistic.

Kees van der Pijl defines the new world order as the globalization of the Lockeian state/society configuration, characterized by the dominance of market forces, historically challenged by a series of 'Hobbesian' contender states trying to catch up with the Lockeian heartland, first on the European continent, then in the rest of the world. Supported by transnational elite networks, the Lockeian system of 'economic freedom' has triumphed; and the current era, the 'second glorious revolution', or 'second great transformation' in Polanyi's terms, seems to be a terminal crisis of the Hobbesian state.

Yoshikazu Sakamoto explores the potential of global democratization against the background of the internationalization and subnationalization of the state. The first of these processes implies an erosion of state power, as the forces of production are increasingly globalized, whereas the latter implies a fragmentation of the state due to the rise of ethnonationalism. There is a gap, he says, between the global problematic and national democracy. These trends make people's power diffuse, unless coupled with the formation of a strong civil society; but, if based on critical social movements, a new perspective on a democratic world order may be generated. For this to be possible, cultural as well as civilizational determinism must be rejected, and a new multilateralism based on cultural pluralism created. Thus, Sakamoto puts his faith in the 'reciprocity' type of response.

To conclude on an optimistic note, it should be noted that, although all the authors in this volume conceive current trends – globalization – in the international political economy as rather distressing, their contributions are not at all gloomy. Cox, in emphasizing also the importance of cultural dimensions of a post-hegemonic world order, speaks of a global 'supra-intersubjectivity' providing a bridge across the subjectivities of different coexisting (and internally transforming) civilizations. This is the vision of post-hegemonic global pluralism. Rosenau says that to allow for the possibility that we may presently be at a turning point in history is to give ourselves licence to exercise control over our future. Gill cites Gramsci's political maxim 'pessimism of the intelligence, optimism of the will' and concludes by observing that not all the symptoms that arise during the interregnum are morbid ones. Van der Pijl points to the 'non-elites', and Sakamoto to popular forces of global democratization, the 'power of the powerless', while my own analysis in this Introduction has pointed to new forms of transnational redistributive polities as well as protective local reciprocity networks, for correcting the dislocations of market utopianism. The international political economy of disorder is also the international political economy of the future.

Notes

1. Some widely used textbooks are Gilpin, 1987; Strange, 1988; Gill and Law, 1988; Spero, 1990; Murphy and Tooze, 1991; Frieden and Lake, 1991; Stubbs and Underhill, 1994. The list of references appended to this introduction also contains a general bibliography with a more comprehensive list of relevant IPE literature.

2. To a large extent the ideas of 'post-conditions' overlap. The 'modern condition' in terms of International Relations theory is the system of territorial states; 'modern territoriality' (Ruggie, 1993) is the Westphalian system *and* the expansion of Europe – the Columbian age. On the other hand, the 'neo-equipment', with the help of which we are supposed to understand the new condition, reflect the same old ideological battlefield. After the hegemony of neo-realism it is time for a neo-idealist revival (Kegley, 1993).

3. The literature on hegemonic decline and its consequences contains different theoretical perspectives and, consequently, different scenarios as far as the post-hegemonic world is concerned. Normally the transition period between two hegemonic systems is, as Modelski (1978) and Gilpin (1981) have emphasized, marked by warfare. Authors on the left tend to make the more apocalyptic forecasts: if war can be avoided, hegemonic decline at least signals a collapse of capitalism (Block, 1977; Mandel, 1974; Wallerstein, 1979). Liberal authors, on the other hand (Rosecrance, 1986), see a substitute in an international trading system consisting of a number of nations realizing that they can better advance their position through economic development and trade than through recourse to war. Conservative authors feel uncomfortable with the concept and its implications for US power (Huntington, 1988). Joseph Nye argues that the USA is bound to lead, but due to what he calls 'complex interdependence' a very special type of leadership is needed (Nye, 1990). The more multidimensional the way hegemonic power is defined, the more difficult it is to answer the question about rise or decline in precise quantitative terms. Decline may characterize one dimension and not another. It is, therefore, unclear at what point it is appropriate to talk of 'after hegemony' (Gill and Law, 1988: 336).

4. A forum for the more mainstream debate is the journal *International Organization* (*IO*). See, for instance, the following articles: J.G. Ruggie, 'International Regimes, Transactions and Change: Embedded Liberalism in the Postwar Economic Order', *IO*, 36, 1982: 379–415; A.A. Stein, 'The Hegemon's Dilemma: Great Britain, the United States, and the International Economic Order', *IO*, 38, 1984: 355–86; B. Russett, 'The Mysterious Case of Vanishing Hegemony, or, Is Mark Twain Really Dead?', *IO*, 39 (2), 1985: 207–31; S. Strange, 'Protectionism and World Politics', *IO*, 39, 1985: 233–59; D. Snidal, 'The Limits of Hegemonic Stability Theory', *IO*, 39, 1985: 579–614; S. Strange, 'The Persistent Myth of Lost Hegemony', *IO*, 41 (4): 551–74, 1987. On the whole, *International Organization* is essential reading if one wishes to understand the intellectual origins of mainstream IPE (Murphy and Tooze, 1991: 4). For the current debate, the UK-based *Review of International Political Economy* should be consulted.

5. Paul Kennedy (1987) explicitly avoids theorizing and provides a historical account of the rise and fall of great powers. He studies the relationship between economic depression and military strength and finds that hegemonic decline is related to what he calls 'imperial overstretch'. Following a critical review of 'declinist literature', the conservative theorist Samuel Huntington (1988: 77) concludes: 'The image of renewal is far closer to the American truth then the image of decadence purveyed by the declinists.' Joseph Nye (1990) argues that the United States remains the dominant power with no challenger to its position in sight. However, the nature of power itself has changed as the world has become more interdependent.

Susan Strange (1988) emphasizes *structural power*, defined through four dimensions: security, production, finance and knowledge; and concludes that the USA retains its position as the leading power in all four dimensions. In particular she criticizes the idea that 'Made in USA' should be taken as an indicator of power. 'What matters is the relation between the United States as a state with political authority and the corporations operating in and outside the United States' (1988: 237). Bruce Russett (1985) similarly makes a distinction between *power base* and *control over outcomes*, and concedes US decline only in the former. Using the Gramscian concept of hegemony, Robert Cox from the 'critical school' of IPE asserts (1987) that the USA may well remain dominant, but still lose hegemonic power. The very fact that US hegemony is called in question indicates a weakening of the ideological dimensions of hegemony. Stephen Gill (1990) finds the debate too nation-centred and emphasizes the internationalization of the USA, and the Americanization of the World: the emergence of a transnational economy, which in later works he calls the global politial economy.

References

Ágh, A. (1990) 'The Hundred Years' Peace: Karl Polanyi on the Dynamics of World Systems', in K. Polanyi-Levitt, *The Life and Work of Karl Polanyi*, Black Rose Books, Montreal, 1990.

Albert, M. (1993) *Capitalism against Capitalism*, Whurr, London.

Ashley, R.K. (1984) 'The Poverty of Neo-Realism', *International Organization*, vol. 38, no. 2, pp. 225–86.

Barry Jones, R.J. (1988) *The Worlds of Political Economy: Alternative Approaches to the Study of Contemporary Political Economy*, Pinter, London and New York.

Block, Fred (1977) *The Origins of International Economic Disorder*, University of California Press, Berkeley.

Blomström, M., and B. Hettne (1984) *Development Theory in Transition. The Dependency Debate and Beyond: Third World Responses*, Zed Books, London.

Brett, E.A. (1985) *The World Economy Since the War: The Politics of Uneven Development*, Macmillan, London.

Brown, Chris (1988) 'Marxist Approaches to International Political Economy', in R.J. Barry Jones, ed., *The Worlds of Political Economy: Alternative Approaches to the Study of Contemporary Political Economy*, Pinter, London and New York.

Bull, H. (1977) *The Anarchical Society. A Study of Order in World Politics*, Columbia University Press, New York.

Buzan, B. (1991) *People, States and Fear: An Agenda for International Security Studies in the Post-Cold War Era*, Harvester Wheatsheaf, Hemel Hempstead.

Caporaso, J.A., and D.P. Levine (1992) *Theories of Poliitical Economy*, Cambridge University Press, New York.

Cox, R.W. (1983) 'Gramsci, Hegemony and International Relations. An Essay in Method', *Millennium*, vol. 12, no. 2 (Summer), pp. 162–75.

—— (1987) *Production, Power, and World Order: Social Forces in the Making of History*, Columbia University Press, New York.

—— (1991) *Perspectives on Multilateralism*, United Nations University, Tokyo.

—— (1993) 'Structural Issues of Global Governance: Implications for Europe', in S. Gill, ed., *Gramsci, Historical Materialism and International Relations*, Cambridge University Press, Cambridge.

—— (1994) 'The Crisis in World Order and the Challenge to International Organization', *Cooperation and Conflict*, vol. 29, no. 2, pp. 99–113.

Frieden, J.A., and D.A. Lake (1991) *International Political Economy. Perspectives on Global Power and Wealth*, Unwin Hyman, London.

Gill, S. (1990) *American Hegemony and the Trilateral Commission*, Cambridge University Press, Cambridge.

Gill, S., ed. (1993) *Gramsci, Historical Materialism and International Relations*, Cambridge University Press, Cambridge.

Gill, S., and D. Law (1988) *The Global Political Economy. Perspectives, Problems and, Policies*, Harvester Wheatsheaf, Hemel Hempstead.

Gilpin, R. (1981) *War and Change in World Politics*, Cambridge University Press, Cambridge.

—— (1987) *The Political Economy of International Relations*, Princeton University Press, Princeton, N.J.

Heilbroner, R.L. (1985) *Nature and Logic of Capitalism*, W.W. Norton, New York.

Hettne, B. (1990) 'The Contemporary Crisis: The Rise of Reciprocity', in K. Polanyi-Levitt, *The Life and Work of Karl Polanyi*, Black Rose Books, Montreal, 1990.

—— (1991) 'Europe and the Crisis: The Regionalist Scenario Revisited', in M. Mendel and D. Salée, eds, *The Legacy of Karl Polanyi. Market, State and Society at the End of the Twentieth Century*, Macmillan, London.

—— (1993a) 'The Concept of Neomercantilism', in L. Magnusson, ed., *Mercantilist Economies*, Kluwer, London.

—— (1993b) 'Neomercantilism: the Pursuit of Regionness', *Cooperation and Conflict*, vol. 28, no. 3, pp. 211–32.

—— (1995) *Development Theory and the Three Worlds: Towards an International Political Economy of Development*, Longman, London.

Hettne, B., and A. Inotai (1994) *The New Regionalism*, WIDER, Helsinki.

Huntington, S.P. (1988) 'The US – Decline or Renewal?', *Foreign Affairs*, vol. 67, no. 2.

Hymer, S. (1972) 'The Multinational Corporation and the Law of Uneven Development', in I.N. Bhagwati, ed., *Economics and World Order*, Collier–Macmillan, London, pp. 113–40.

Kegley, C.W. (1993) 'The Neo-idealist Moment in International Studies? Realist Myths and the New International Realities', *International Studies Quarterly*, vol. 37, no. 2 (June).

Kennedy, P. (1987) *The Rise and Fall of the Great Powers*, Random House, New York.

Keohane, R.O. (1980) 'The Theory of Hegemonic Stability and Changes in International Economic Regimes, 1966–77', in O.R. Holsti, R.M. Siversen, and A.L. George, eds, *Change in the International System*, Westview, Boulder, Colo.

——— (1984) *After Hegemony: Cooperation and Discord in the World Political Economy*, Princeton University Press, Princeton, N.J.

——— (1989) *International Institutions and State Power*, Westview Press, Boulder, Colo.

Keohane, R.O., ed. (1986) *Neo-realism and its Critics*, Columbia University Press, New York.

Keohane, R.O., and J. Nye, (1977) *Power and Interdependence*, Little, Brown, Boston.

Kindleberger, C. (1973) *The World in Depression*, University of California Press, Berkeley.

Krasner, S.D. (1985) *Structural Conflict: The Third World Against Global Liberalism*, University of California Press, Berkeley, Los Angeles, London.

Krasner, S.D., ed. (1982) 'International Regimes', special issue of *International Organization*, vol. 36, no. 2.

Lipietz, Alain (1993) *Towards a New Economic Order. Postfordism, Ecology and Democracy*, Polity Press, Cambridge.

McGrew, A.G., and P.G. Lewis, eds (1992) *Global Politics. Globalization and the Nation-State*, Polity Press, Cambridge.

Mendell, M., and D. Salée, eds (1991) *The Legacy of Karl Polanyi. Market, State and Society at the End of the Twentieth Century*, Macmillan, London.

Modelski, G. (1978) 'The Long Cycle of Global Politics and the Nation-State', *Comparative Studies in Society and History*, vol. 20, April 1978.

Murphy, C.N., and R. Tooze, eds (1991) *The New International Political Economy*, Lynne Rienner, Boulder, Colo.; Macmillan, London.

Nye, J.S. (1990) *Bound to Lead: the Changing Nature of American Power*, Basic Books, New York.

Ougaard, M. (1988) 'Dimensions of Hegemony', *Cooperation and Conflict*, XXIII, pp. 197–214.

Peterson, V.S., and A. Sisson Runyan (1993) *Global Gender Issues*, Westview Press, Boulder, Colo.

Polanyi, Karl (1945) 'Universal Capitalism or Regional Planning', *The London Quarterly of World Affairs*.

——— (1957) *The Great Transformation* [1944], Beacon Press, Boston.

Polanyi-Levitt, K. (1990) *The Life and Work of Karl Polanyi*, Black Rose Books, Montreal.

Robertson, R. (1992) *Globalization. Social Theories and Global Culture*, Sage, London.

Rosecrance, R. (1986) *The Rise of the Trading State*, Basic Books, New York.

Rosenau, J.N. (1990) *Turbulence in World Politics. A Theory of Change and Continuity*, Princeton University Press, Princeton, N.J.

Rosenau, J.N., and H. Tromp, eds (1989) *Interdependence and Conflict in World Politics*, Avebury, Aldershot.

Ruggie, J.G. (1983) 'International Regimes, Transactions and Change: Embedded Liberalism in the Postwar Economic Order', in D.S. Krasner, ed., *International Regimes*, Cornell University Press, Ithaca, N.Y.

———— (1986) 'Continuity and Transformation in the World Polity: Toward a Neorealist Synthesis', in R.O. Keohane, ed., *Neorealism and its Critics*, Columbia University Press, New York.

———— (1993) 'Territoriality and Beyond: Problematizing Modernity in International Relations', *International Organization*, vol. 47, no. 1 (Winter), pp. 139–74.

Russet, B. (1985) 'The Mysterious Case of Vanishing Hegemony; or Is Mark Twain Really Dead?', *International Organization*, vol. 39, no. 2, pp. 207–31.

Sakamoto, Y., ed. (1994) *Global Transformation*, United Nations University Press, Tokyo.

Scholte, J.A. (1993), *International Relations and Social Change*, Open University Press, Milton Keynes.

Shaw, Martin (1994) *Global Society and International Relations*, Polity Press, Cambridge.

Skocpol, T. (1984) *Vision and Method in Historical Sociology*, Cambridge University Press, Cambridge.

Sörensen, G, (1994) 'International Relations after the Cold War: What has changed? Toward a theory of units', mimeo, School of International Relations and Pacific Studies, University of California, San Diego.

Spero, J. (1990) *The Politics of International Economic Relations*, Allen & Unwin, London; St Martin's Press, New York.

Staniland, Martin (1985) *What is Political Economy? A Study of Social Theory and Underdevelopment*, Yale University Press, New Haven and London.

Strange, S. (1985) 'Protectionism and World Politics', *International Organization*, vol. 39, no. 2, pp. 233–59.

———— (1987) 'The Persistent Myth of Lost Hegemony', *International Organization*, vol. 41, no. 4, pp. 551–74.

———— (1988) *States and Markets*, Pinter, London and New York.

Stubbs, R., and G. Underhill, eds (1994) *Political Economy and the Changing Global Order*, Macmillan, London.

Tooze, R. (1988) 'Liberal International Political Economy', in R.J. Barry Jones, ed., *The Worlds of Political Economy: Alternative Approaches to the Study of Contemporary Political Economy*, Pinter, London and New York.

Vincent, R.J. (1983) 'Change and International Relations', *Review of International Studies* 9.

Wallerstein, I. (1979) *The Capitalist World Economy*, Cambridge University Press, Cambridge.

———— (1991) *Unthinking Social Science. The Limits of Nineteenth-Century Paradigms*, Polity Press, Cambridge.

2

Critical Political Economy
Robert W. Cox

Preface

My task in this chapter is to discuss how to approach the study of political economy in the context of global structural changes. As a preliminary, I should make clear my position on some basic points: (i) the role of theory; (ii) the meaning of political economy; (iii) its basic components, or ontology; and (iv) how to study change.

Theory

First of all, there is no theory in itself, no theory independent of a concrete historical context. Theory is the way the mind works to understand the reality it confronts. It is the self-consciousness of that mind, the awareness of how facts experienced are perceived and organized so as to be understood. Theory thus follows reality in the sense that it is shaped by the world of experience. But it also precedes the making of reality in that it orients the minds of those who by their actions reproduce or change that reality.

Theory is always *for* someone and *for* some purpose. We need to know the context in which theory is produced and used; and we need to know whether the aim of the user is to maintain the existing social order or to change it. These two purposes lead to two kinds of theory. What I shall call 'problem-solving' theory takes the world as given (and on the whole as good) and provides guidance to correct dysfunctions or specific problems that arise within this existing order. The other kind of theory, which I shall call 'critical' (although I do not thereby affiliate with any particular tendencies that have heretofore adopted that word) is concerned with how the existing order came into being and what the possibilities are for change in that order. The first is concerned with specific reforms aimed at the maintenance of existing structures, the second with exploring the potential for structural change and the construction of strategies for change.

Political economy

The next question is: change in what? What is political economy? I suggest that political economy is different from both political science and economics as they are commonly understood. We sometimes hear international political economy defined as the politics of international economic relations. This suggests an amalgam or *rapprochement* of the two fields.

Yet there is a methodological difference between political science and economics, on the one hand, and political economy, as I would like to define it, on the other. Political science and economics are actor-oriented studies. They take off from some rather fixed assumptions about the framework or parameters within which actions take place – the institutional framework of politics, or the concept of the market. Within these parameters, they can often give quite precise answers to specific questions. Political scientists can analyse political processes within existing structures and possibly give useful advice to politicians about how to gain or retain office or what policy options are feasible in terms of public support. Economists use the relationships derived from the rather abstract concept of a market to predict outcomes under different conditions. Both provide examples of the application of problem-solving theory.

Political economy, by contrast, is concerned with the historically constituted frameworks or structures within which political and economic activity takes place. It stands back from the apparent fixity of the present to ask how the existing structures came into being and how they may be changing, or how they may be induced to change. In this sense, political economy is critical theory.

Historical structures

There is, of course, no absolute distinction between actors and
structures. It is not a question of sacrificing the one or the other.
Structures are formed by collective human activity over time. Structures, in turn, mould the thoughts and actions of individuals.
Historical change is to be thought of as the reciprocal relationship
of structures and actors. There is a difference, however, between
thinking of this actor–structure relationship as a process configuring
structural change, and thinking of actions as confined within fixed,
given structures in the manner of problem-solving theory.

The notion of a framework for action or historical structure is
a picture of a particular configuration of forces. This configuration
does not determine actions in any direct, mechanical way but
imposes pressures and constraints. Individuals and groups may
move with the pressures or resist and oppose them, but they cannot ignore them. To the extent that they do successfully resist a
prevailing historical structure they buttress their actions with an
alternative, emerging configuration of forces, a rival structure.

Intersubjective meanings

A structure, as I have suggested, is a picture of reality, of the
world, or of that aspect of the world that impresses itself upon us
at any particular time – the power relations among nations, or
those of the workplace, or of the family or local community. This
picture, shared among many people, defines reality for them; and
because they think of reality in the same way, their actions and
words tend to reproduce this reality. These realities go by various
names – the state, the family, the job market, and so forth. It does
not matter whether we approve or disapprove of these realities.
They constitute the world in which we live. They are the parameters of our existence. Knowing them to be there means knowing
that other people will act as though they are there, even though
none of these entities exists as a physical thing. There is no clean
separation between objectivity ('out there') and subjectivity (in the
mind). The ontology which defines the 'real world', the world of

non-physical realities that shape our existence, is sustained by intersubjective meanings derived from long years of collective experience.

This intersubjective making of reality is not a statement of philosophical idealism. These intersubjectively constituted entities have been created by collective human responses to the material conditions of human existence over long periods of time. The state is a historical creation, a response to certain conditions, even though it may appear as an immutable reality. Critical theory examines the origins of the state, of particular historical forms of state. Critical theorists look into forces that may be changing the nature of the state and the inter-state system. (Feminists have enquired into the gendered character of states.)

The configuration of intersubjectively constituted entities we can call, borrowing a philosophical term, an ontology. For each era and each object of interest there is a relevant ontology. Ontologies tell us what is significant in the particular worlds we delve into – what are the basic entities and the key relationships. Ontologies are not arbitrary constructions; they are the specification of the common sense of an epoch. So we will need to establish the ontology relevant to a study of world political economy in the late twentieth century.

Change

We need also to go beyond the ontology of a particular time to find the mental tools capable of understanding change in historical structures. Ontology gives us a synchronic view of reality. It lays out the entities and relationships that are the key to understanding what happens in a particular sector of human activity at a particular historical juncture. Social science has done a reasonably good job of understanding the synchronic dimension of human affairs. Functionalism, Max Weber's ideal types, Marx's capitalist mode of production, are all tools for understanding the synchronic.

The problem of structural change – the diachronic dimension – has been less successfully dealt with. Broadly, there have been three approaches. One is extrapolation. You take what appear to be the dominant tendencies in the present and project them into the future. This is a way of saying that the future will be like the present, only more so. A second approach is to deny that change can be understood, which means that we have to think in terms of a disconnected sequence of synchronic structures, being unable to explain the movement from one to the next. I think some aspects of postmodernism fall into this category, though I stand to be corrected. The third approach – and the one which seems most convincing to me – is historical dialectic. Each historical structure, depicted synchronically, contains both coherence (without which it would not be a structure) and elements of contradiction or conflict. Structural transformation comes from developments out of these points of conflict. Contrasting alternative structures arise within existing dominant structures. In some cases, they displace the formerly dominant structures, retaining some of their features and transforming others. Thus, the synchronic and the diachronic can be merged. Among those who have most effectively pursued this approach, I would single out Antonio Gramsci, Karl Polanyi, and Fernand Braudel. It is worth pointing out that these three were concerned with strategy as well as with analysis. As someone once said, the purpose of understanding the world is to be better able to change it.

Let me summarize this rather abstract preface: (i) Theory is time-bound and derived from historical experience. Problem-solving theory helps to maintain the existing order. Critical theory is an aid to changing it. (ii) Political economy is a form of critical theory. It analyses historical structures which are the ways reality is defined for different peoples in different eras – that is, the frameworks within which people interact with nature for the satisfaction of their needs. (iii) Reality is made by the collective responses of people to the conditions of their existence. Intersubjectively shared experience reproduces reality in the form of continuing institutions and practices. (iv) Change is to be understood dialectically; that is, each successive historical structure generates the contradictions and points of conflict that bring about its transformation.

An Ontological Shift?

The first task of a contemporary political economy is to reveal its ontology. One widely circulated ontological picture is the 'end of history' thesis associated with Francis Fukuyama. It envisages a world in which formerly conflicting realities have converged into a single model: the apotheosis of capitalism and formal liberal democracy. This vision expresses the ultimate triumph of the Enlightenment, of modernism, of European civilization. John Kenneth Galbraith, who is uncomfortable with it, calls this the 'culture of contentment', a vision retained by the relatively privileged few.

As against this, there is the perception that decay is evident and widespread: social polarization on both global and domestic levels; depoliticization and non-participation that undermine the legitimacy of political institutions, and which extend from contempt for the political classes in evolved pluralistic societies to a perception of the state as enemy of the people in less fortunate countries that have known repressive dictatorships. Stirring within this decaying legitimacy are various movements of identity and protest, some seeking to reinvent democracy, others steeped in a new authoritarianism.

This complex movement of negation is to be found in all parts of the world – in Italy and Japan as well as in Somalia and Liberia. It opens a void in intersubjectivity that foreshadows an ontological shift, the displacement of the old realism while a new realism is as yet only latent. The ontological shift is apparent in all major aspects of world political economy: (i) in the prospect of a post-Westphalian political order; (ii) in the restructuring of global society and reactions to the consequences of economic globalization; (iii) in the intervention of the biosphere into world politics; and (iv) in the implications of a multicultural post-hegemonic world order.

A post-Westphalian political order?

One of Hedley Bull's speculations about possible future world orders was what he called a 'new medievalism'. This envisages a complex multilevel world formed by a combination of macroregions (like the European Community), the perpetuation of many existing states with limited sovereignties, the disintegration of some existing states into autonomous micro-regions (Catalonia, Croatia, Quebec, and so on), transnational firms and social and religious movements analogous to medieval corporations and religious orders, global communications networks, and ever-integrating technologies.

Bull was sceptical whether the observable tendencies in these directions would efface the state system as the centrepiece of world politics. The concepts and vocabulary of the state system are, after all, still used by those who promote the disintegration of existing states and new territorially based autonomies. Nor did he think such a multilevel order would be less prone to violence than the world society of states that he perceived as the development of the Westphalian system. Yet this is the image that most merits reflection as a possible description of future world politics.

There is, of course, no question of the state disappearing. Yet if we follow up the realist question 'Where does power lie?' we have to rethink conventional answers. States are not alike. The entity we call 'the state' is a complex of governmental functions and societal practices. There are different forms of state, or different state/society complexes. Then, in addition, there are various more or less formal and permanent linkages binding some states or parts of states, and a variety of economic or business organizations, social movements, and religious or ethnic or ideological movements that intervene in world politics.

One of the principal factors to be taken into account in defining the ontology of future world political economy is the reshaping of capitalism during the post-Cold War period. During the 1980s, a hyper-liberal form of capitalism gained ascendency, spreading from America and Britain over much of the world. It is characterized by a liberating of the private sector from state intervention. This particular relationship of state to society has been propagated by the institutions of the world economy (the IMF and World Bank) in the countries of Africa and Latin America caught in a debt trap. It was embraced by countries of the former Soviet bloc as the fast track to capitalism.

In the early 1990s, doubts and caution about hyper-liberal

capitalism gained ground with lagging growth, increasing polarization of rich and poor, and environmental degradation. Hyper-
liberalism won converts in Western European business circles, but
it also encountered an older and more deeply entrenched tradition
of social-market or social-democratic capitalism. The current issues
over the future of Europe such as the question of a common
currency, of 'subsidiarity', and of how far Europe can go beyond
a trade agreement, fall into place as aspects of the broader question:
What kind of state/society complex is for Europe? The 'social
Europe' of the social-democratic left is very different from the
Thatcherite view of an economic agreement facilitating trade and
capital movements sheltered from political intervention. The issue
will not be resolved in the short term by a treaty or a referendum.
It will be decided in a long-term struggle among social forces.

Similarly, Japanese capitalism is evolving in its own manner, and
the expanding capitalisms of East Asia model themselves more on
the Japanese, in a close relationship of capital to state, than on
American or European capitalisms. The future world pattern of
economic organization is not likely to take the form of a single
dominant global capitalism, but rather of three or more types of
substantive economy manoeuvring to achieve a *modus vivendi*.

The emerging economic centres of power are unlike the territorial economic blocs of the 1930s. They are not conceived as
autarkic, inward directed and isolated from the rest of the world.
Rather they are concentrations of economic power, more readily
identified with cities than with states, that use the political leverage
of states to compete more effectively for world market shares.
These are, in Susan Strange's words, 'non-territorial empires' over-
lapping geographically, accumulating power of decision, power of
choice, in a few centres by drawing resources from their global
networks.

Moreover, these centres of political–economic authority are
under pressure from social forces. The intensity of social pressures
differs among these poles of economic power. On a present reading, it would seem greatest in Europe, less in North America, and
least in East Asia. The nature of social conflict is also shifting
from the nineteenth- and early-twentieth-century paradigm of class

struggle. Of course, class struggle continues in the sense of a cleavage of dominant and subordinate social groups; but the self-consciousness of subordinate social groups has often become fragmented into different identities characterized by ethnicity, religion or gender. Here, as elsewhere, the ontological shift is also a shift in intersubjectivities.

Post-globalization?

Let us look more closely at the struggle of social forces as it is being shaped by economic globalization, for this may prove to be the underlying factor in the constitution of future political authorities and future world order.

Karl Polanyi's analysis of capitalism in the nineteenth and twentieth centuries showed a dialectical process that he called the 'double movement'. The first phase of that process was an attempt to impose a utopia called the self-regulating market. The project was to disembed the economy from society so as to allow the market to function without social or political constraints, in effect to make it a dominant and unrestricted power over society. This project failed as society reacted to bring the market under social and political control, beginning with factory legislation, social insurance and the institutionalizing of industrial relations, and culminating in the welfare state.

Polanyi has given us a framework for thinking about the prospects of the current project of neo-liberalism in the global economy. The key criterion today is competitiveness; and derived from that are universal imperatives of deregulation, privatization, and the restriction of public intervention in economic processes. Neo-liberalism is transforming states from being buffers between external economic forces and the domestic economy into agencies for adapting domestic economies to the exigencies of the global economy. So now the market appears to be bursting free from the bonds of national societies, to subject global society to its laws. The results on the global level are like those Polanyi saw in nineteenth-century Britain: greater polarization of rich and poor, disintegration of pre-existing social bonds, and alienation.

The logic of Polanyi's analysis leads us to look for the sources of opposition to the effects of economic globalization, and the possible emergence of a more coherent countervailing force and an alternative theory of social and economic organization. Theory will grow both as a by-product of struggle and as an aid in struggle. It will derive from reflection upon accumulating experience, and will organize the understanding of experience in new ontologies and new strategies.

Among the many sources of disruption in global society out of which the countermovement may come, a few stand out. One is the restructuring of production. The dominant segment of the global economy has globalized production of goods and services. Whether in automobiles or data processing, national boundaries have become subordinate to the rationality of global production processes. These processes are no longer circumscribed within the bureaucracies of big multinational corporations, but are increasingly managed by more flexible networks of productive entities composed and recomposed around specific projects.

One consequence is that the core/periphery metaphor, which had a geographical connotation describing the dominant–subordinate relationship of national economies, now applies more accurately to a social relationship. The new production organizations have a relatively small core of permanent employees, and a larger number of peripheral employees whose relationship to the production network is more precarious. Moreover, this peripheral body of employees is fragmented (segmented is the word more commonly used by labour economists) into distinct groups separated by location, by ethnicity, and by gender. One obvious result has been the weakening of the cohesion and power of the labour movement.

A second consequence has been the marginalization of a large part of the world's population which is not effectively integrated within the global economy. It has become manifest that the link between production and jobs has been broken in the restructuring of production. In some of the rich countries beset by the recession, we hear of the prospect of a jobless recovery. Project that on a world scale and you get the prospect of a large population superfluous to the global production process, much but certainly not all

of it in Third World countries. The cleavage between the integrated and the superfluous in Third World countries is illustrated
when the most fertile lands are given over to export crops, while
desertification and famine attack subsistence farmers, who incidentally happen in most cases to be women. The power relations
created by the global economy are very clear, and peasant women
are near the bottom of the scale.

The perception that much of the world's population is not
needed by the global economy seems to have been recognized
implicitly (though never openly) by the principal world institutions.
Policies to promote economic development have been very largely
displaced in favour of what can be called global poor relief and
riot control. Poor societies that are unlikely to contribute to the
global economy should be prevented from disrupting its growth.
Fantu Cheru has used the term 'global apartheid'. It is striking to
see how the United Nations has cut back development assistance
to put its main emphasis on humanitarian relief and military intervention – this in marked contrast to the policies of the 1960s.

A third consequence, the logical result of the second, is mass
migration from South to North and from East to West. Figures
for people now on the move range from 60 to 100 million. Pre-
sumably nobody really knows. The absolute numbers are large, yet
only a small fraction of world population. What is significant is the
rate of increase and the perceptions of threat aroused in the richer
receiving countries while they suffer through recession. The migration issue has moved to the centre of the political agenda and has
provoked sentiments both of generosity and of aggressiveness in
the receiving countries, giving an emotional charge to opposed
visions of a future society.

The biosphere

Another consequence of economic globalization has been environmental destruction. There are two aspects to the problem. One is
in relations among peoples. The aggressive search for resources by
economically dominant interests and the off-loading of polluting
and energy-intensive processes to newly industrializing countries

has resulted in a kind of environmental neo-colonialism – the dominant societies clean up and move to more knowledge-intensive production while those following in their tracks become sites of environmental degradation.

The aspect of relations among peoples has also been seen as a trade-off between environment and development. Rich countries have appropriated most of the world's non-renewable resources and done most of the polluting. Poor countries respond to the rich countries' efforts to press environmentalism upon the poor by demanding some support for their aspirations to become wealthier. If they are to be precluded from doing what the rich have already done to the environment, they expect some compensation. Attempts to resolve this trade-off, most recently at the Earth Summit in Brazil during 1992, have been, to say the least, inconclusive.

The other aspect of the environmental problem, and perhaps in the long run the more important, concerns the relationship of human organization to nature. 'Environment' is an inappropriate term here, since it suggests a separation between human activity, on the one hand, and the environment as a kind of passive substance that suffers the impact of human practices, on the other. The biosphere is a better concept, since it places human practices alongside other forms of life in an interdependent relationship. Aggressiveness in human practices within the biosphere are met with active response by non-human elements. Global warming, the hole in the ozone layer, the decline of world fish stocks, become active forces in world politics.

Social practices are called in question. Is it conceivable that the populations of China and the Third World could consume in the same manner and at the same rate as the populations of North America and Europe without provoking collapse of the biosphere? Of course, given the social bias in economic globalization, this may be an unlikely prospect. But the question challenges the developmental and consumption models of economic globalization. President George Bush was reported as saying, apropos of last summer's Earth Summit: 'Our lifestyle is not up for negotiation.' This is consistent with the perspective of immediacy characteristic of politicians in an election campaign; but it may also reflect a distant awareness that the issue remains unresolved. The relatively affluent are challenged to rethink their patterns of consumption and behaviour, in relation to the biosphere and to the models they project to less affluent peoples.

Post-hegemony?

The question of consumption models is closely linked to the question of hegemony. In the terms I have used, an indicator of hegemony would be a preponderant ontology that tends to absorb or subordinate all others. One intersubjective understanding of the world excludes all others and appears to be universal. It is often said that although United States economic power in the world has experienced a relative decline, the American way of life has never been a more powerful model. An American-derived 'business civilization', to use Susan Strange's term, characterizes the globalizing elites; and American pop culture has projected an image of the good life that is a universal object of emulation – a universalized model of consumption. This constitutes a serious obstacle to the rethinking of social practices so as to be more compatible with the biosphere.

A counterchallenge to the universalizing of American pop culture is the affirmation of other cultural identities. The most evident, and the most explicitly negating of American culture, is in Islam; but other cultures are also affirming alternative world-views. The hegemonies of the past and present have universalized from one national culture or one tradition of civilization. A post-hegemonic world order would no longer be the global reach of one particular form of civilization. It would contain a plurality of visions of world order.

In order to avoid such an order lapsing into mutual incomprehension and conflict, it would be necessary to move beyond a position of pure relativism in order to achieve a kind of supraintersubjectivity that would provide a bridge across the distinct and separate subjectivities of the different coexisting civilizations.

These various traditions of civilization are not monolithic and fixed. They develop dialectically like any historical structure. Change may come both from internal contradictions – for example, gendered power relations and social inequities can be sources of conflict and mutation in all cultures. Change can also come from borrowings and reactions to the practices of other cultures in a world that is becoming ever more closely knit. Selective adaptation rather than homogenization would characterize change in post-hegemonic pluralism.

Towards a Common Moral Philosophy

All of the developments I have discussed point to a global process of decomposition and recomposition of civil societies and political authorities which is more profound than tinkering and reforms by elites, and involves movements emanating from the base of society. This raises the most basic philosophical and political issues of a cross-cultural and cross-civilizational kind.

Modern Western political culture is rooted in a political, economic, philosophical and methodological individualism. 'Globalization' is its ultimate expression. The roots of it are perhaps best represented in Adam Smith's reflection that '[I]t is not from the benevolence of the butcher, the brewer, or the baker that we expect our dinner, but from their regard to their own interest.' Smith was characteristic of much eighteenth-century European thought in hypothesizing an 'invisible hand' that mysteriously led the pursuit of private interests to result unintentionally in public good. Hegel's 'ruse of reason' was another manifestation of this eighteenth-century refurbishing in secular terms of an older Christian doctrine of Divine Providence.

There was, of course, another aspect to Smith: the Scottish moral philosopher, who emphasized the social propensities of men existing alongside the selfish; but this has been ignored by classical economics. The ultimate extreme, indeed travesty, of the possessive individualist side of Smith is to be found in the affirmation attributed to Margaret Thatcher that there is no such thing as society; there are only individuals. This is perhaps not to be taken seriously as philosophy, but it does epitomize much current ideology.

The reconstitution of society and political authority from the bottom up would require a different sense of the polity: one that put emphasis on arousing capacities for collective action inspired by common purposes. There is another and older tradition of thought which evokes collective sentiments. This tradition enquires into the conditions for the existence of cohesion and common purpose in society. It perceives that these sentiments actually constitute society as something distinct from the aggregation of individuals pursuing their separate interests. It distinguishes creative eras of political and social construction from eras of disintegration and decay of public spirit.

This kind of political thought has appeared in civilizations outside the modern West; it has also appeared in the West in earlier times and has survived through modernity as an alternative undercurrent of Western thought. The fourteenth-century Islamic historian and diplomat Ibn Khaldun called this quality *'asabiya*, by which he meant that sense of solidarity in a group which makes possible the founding of a state. For Ibn Khaldun, this was something that arose and declined in the course of history, distinguishing eras of creativity in human organization from eras of disintegration and decline. In the West, Machiavelli revived from Roman times the concept of *virtù*, which has analogies to *'asabiya* as the moral quality required to create and develop a political community. In early-eighteenth-century Naples, a city at the crossroads of civilizations, Giambattista Vico also addressed the problem of rise and decline. The final stage of decline, characterized by the unconstrained pursuit of factionalism and private interests, he called 'barbarism of reflection'.

The possibility of reconstructing civil society and political authority 'from below' rests upon a revival of the sense of collective responsibility and cross-cultural understanding. Awareness of the problem is a first step. The rest must flow from the experience of many creative social movements.

3

Distant Proximities: The Dynamics and Dialectics of Globalization

James N. Rosenau

It has become quite commonplace to stress the large degree to which powerful communications and transportation technologies are rendering the world ever more interdependent. Public officials, journalists, academics, and a host of others who assess the global scene, refer repeatedly to the vast changes that have ensued as the world gets smaller. And well they might. Social, economic, political and cultural distances are shrinking. The world economy is driving local and national markets. The English language has become the world's lingua franca, just as the artefacts of capitalist culture are everywhere challenging native tastes and customs. The boundaries that divide local, national and international communities are eroding. In short, today a development in any part of the world can have consequences for every other part. What is distant is also proximate, paradoxical as that may seem. The chaos theorists who describe how a butterfly flapping its wings over Brazil can affect the weather over Chicago have identified a process that nicely captures this paradox inherent in the globalization that is transforming world affairs late in the twentieth century.

A Suggestive Metaphor

Let me suggest the significance of the transforming processes with a simple metaphor. By juxtaposing two photographs, both of recent origin but already widely heralded, it is possible to grasp metaphorically the central tension presently racking world affairs. One is a picture of the earth taken from the moon, a blue sphere seemingly suspended in timelessness and expressive of the large extent to which all humans are confined to the same limited space and thus bound by the same vulnerabilities. The other is an intra-uterine photograph of a foetus, the beginning of a life set to evolve its own identity and to trace its own unique course. Put the pictures next to each other and you get a sense of how modern technologies have intensified pressures toward *both* globalization and localization, thus fostering centralizing and decentralizing dynamics that are simultaneously reinforcing and offsetting tendencies toward *both* large-scale coherence and narrow individualism.

But the significance of technology does not lie in the triumphs of aerial and miniaturized photography. Prior generations have also looked where none have seen before. Rather, it is the contents of the two pictures that are so consequential. One tells us more vividly than ever before that all people share a common fate, and the other says no less poignantly that every person has a separate being. Those are powerful messages. They frame thought, stimulate action, give meaning to aspiration. And through still other communications technologies, these messages are circulated repeatedly on a worldwide scale. As such, as widely shared new images of ourselves, they are both sources and reflections of where the centralizing and decentralizing tendencies at work in the world are headed – toward global and regional institutions on the one hand, and toward community, household or individual interests on the other. They are, in short, contradictory images that signify permanence and fragility, universality and diversity, continuity and change. More than that, they are images that feed off each other, with every increment in the clarity of one tending to foster comparable increments in the salience of the other. In the words of one observer, the dynamism of this causal web can be captured by referring to 'globalization and its corollary, domestic fragmentation'.[2]

Powerful and contradictory as the two photographs may be, moreover, neither is as objective a picture as it seems at first glance. Upon close inspection each conveys a diverse set of images, depending upon who is looking at them. For some the earth is not so much a blue sphere as it is a vast market. For others it is shrouded in smog and seems a vulnerable planet. For still others it appears as a whole fragmented into some 183 divisive parts, just as some may view it as embracing pockets of like-minded publics reaching out across the 183 state boundaries for collaboration on behalf of shared values. Similarly, for some the intra-uterine picture is not so much the beginning of an autonomous individual as it is that of a lonely figure destined for a tough, underprivileged life. For others it depicts a fellow citizen. For still others it suggests an aggressive, self-serving person, or an heir in a subsequent generation, or still another addition to an adversary's growing membership.

If we extend the metaphor one step further and assume that it is virtually impossible in today's world not to be familiar with the images and implications inherent in the juxtaposition of the two photographs, clearly people everywhere are confronted with a choice – or, more accurately, with an endless series of choices – between the opportunities offered by large-scale cooperation that may be global in scope and the benefits derived from small-scale organizations that may better serve individual needs and wants. Symbolically speaking, in other words, the two photographs are saying 'Choose!' – decide whether to cohere or to fragment; or, if you can, choose to pursue both wider and narrower goals.

But metaphoric analysis can extend understanding only so far. It can be suggestive but not incisive, hinting at relationships but not revealing their workings. Consequently, clarifying and insightful as the juxtaposed photographs are, they cannot serve as more than a signpost on the route to understanding. They provide no clues as to the direction or intensity of, or differences among, the various processes and structures that are transforming world affairs and complicating the task of observers and policy-makers alike. For that – for enquiry that lifts our understanding to a more precise and encompassing plain – we have to move on to a different kind of analysis, one that requires us to turn on ourselves, to suppress our metaphors, to resist our intuitions, to contain our preferences, and most of all to be self-conscious about our role as observers of the global scene. We need, in effect, to become theoreticians, to organize our observations so that underlying patterns can be discerned and the opportunities they offer for innovative policy seized and applied.

The Dialectics of Globalization and Localization

Such is the purpose of the ensuing inquiry. It seeks to examine systematically some of the phenomena suggested by the metaphor and, in so doing, to demonstrate also the virtues of the theory-building enterprise. More precisely, what follows undertakes to probe two profound dynamics and an even more profound dialectic. One dynamic, implicit in the photograph of the earth taken from the moon, is that of globalization – all those forces that impel individuals, groups, societies and transnational organizations toward more encompassing and coherent forms of centralization and integration. The other dynamic, hinted at by the photo of the intra-uterine foetus, is that of localization – all those pressures that lead people, groups and transnational organizations to narrow their horizons and withdraw in decentralizing and possibly disintegrating directions. Viewed in narrow political terms, globalizing and centralizing processes are conceived to be any developments that facilitate the expansion of authority, activities and interests beyond the existing (usually national) territorial boundaries, whereas localizing and decentralizing processes involve any developments in which the scope of authority and action undergoes contraction and reverts to concerns, issues, groups and/or institutions that are less encompassing than the prevailing territorial or socially constructed boundaries.[3]

It must be stressed that both globalization and localization are conceived as processes which promote and culminate in change. Neither is static. Globalization is not the equivalent of everything that happens on a global scale, and localization does not refer to all the activities that occur at local levels. Rather, both concepts specify a dynamic process in which movement occurs: as it unfolds, globalization fosters more globalization, thus expanding the scope of the global activities; just as localization conduces to more localization as it ensues, thereby contracting the space within which local activities transpire. The extension of markets, the proliferation of satellite dishes that widen television audiences, the spread of social movements, the growth of tourism, the westward or northern flow of people seeking work or asylum, an increase in the frequency of domestic elections monitored by international organizations, the continued institutionalization of the European Community – these exemplify globalizing tendencies; whereas constant levels of international trade, television viewing, movement membership, tourism, migration, election monitoring, and routinized administration within the EC are illustrative of activities on a global scale that simply repeat prior activities and, as such, are static. Similarly, the breakdown of marriages and families, the restructuring of organizations that transfer functions from headquarters to field offices, the advent of breakaway provinces, unions or factions, the growth of cottage industries, the resurgence of native cultures – trends such as these exemplify localizing tendencies. To analyse globalizing and localizing processes, in short, is to observe a world in motion, an expanding and contracting blur of changing orientations, organizations, institutions and patterns that transform the ways in which people conduct their affairs.

Considered in a short time perspective, both the globalizing and localizing dynamics can be viewed as deriving in part from independent sources. At any moment in time the expansion of markets, the onset of pervasive environmental problems, the spread of new technologies for the electronic transfer of money, ideas and pictures, and a host of other factors sustain the processes of globalization irrespective of the historical precedents designed to maintain local and national controls over the pace and direction of change. Likewise, at that same moment in time the psychic comfort from close-at-hand ties and loyalties, the habits inherent in long-standing native cultures, and the unique features of the immediate neighbourhood are among the many factors propelling the processes of localization. Leaving aside their long-term consequences, in other words, the globalizing and localizing dynamics are to some degree independent of each other in the short term. Some of the pressures for change in each dynamic continue irrespective of the counter-pressures exerted by the other.

On the other hand, neither set of dynamics is fully independent. In recent years ever more numerous occasions have arisen when the dynamics have interacted directly and, in effect, operated as causal sources of each other. From a short-term perspective, moreover, this interaction appears to have acquired a momentum of its own. And as the pace increases, as new increments of globalization foster new increments of localization, and vice versa, enormous social and political power is unleashed. Indeed, moving as they do in opposite directions, the interactive dynamics foster many of the conflicts that crowd the global agenda – the tensions between those who would conserve and develop natural resources, between transnational social movements and national governments, between domestic trade unions and migratory labour, between the norms of historic cultures and those of global television, between domestic and imported products, and so on across all the realms of human endeavour.

The question arises as to whether any consistency attaches to the enormous power that derives from the links between globalizing and localizing tendencies. Do the links merely establish a continuous process of dynamic interaction that, depending on unique circumstances, can move history along any one of numerous paths? Or are they founded on underlying tendencies that infuse direction into the course of events and can thus be anticipated?

Given a theoretical predisposition to view human experience as rooted in a larger order that accords coherence to history, a positive answer to this last question can be reasonably developed. It requires two conceptual twists. First, the time perspective must be lengthened beyond the short run so that the interactive dynamics are viewed as part of a long-term process. Second, and more important, a position has to be taken as to whether in a broader context of time the dynamics of globalization occur prior to, and underlie, those of localization. If so, if the enormous power of their interaction is driven by such a central tendency, then the dynamism embedded in their causal links is more than simply an interactive process; rather, it can be seen as constituting a dialectical process in which major increments of globalization contain the seeds of localization that, in turn, reshape the globalizing dynamic.

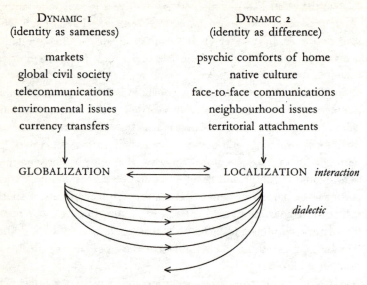

Table 3.1   The Dynamics and Dialectics of Globalization

Attributing primary causal power to globalization is not difficult. For a broad array of reasons, recorded human experience is a history of expanding horizons, of individuals, families, tribes and societies driven by technology and industrialization to move into increasingly coherent and encompassing forms of social, economic and political organization. No less historically conspicuous than the movement along these lines have been the resistances to the globalizing dynamics, counter-reactions driven by the need for identity and the psychic comforts of shared territory and culture to retreat into narrower forms of social, economic and political organization, all of which can be seen as localizing processes that infuse further fragmentation into the course of events. Considered across long stretches of time, in short, the interactive dynamics consist of globalizing theses that give rise to localizing antitheses which foster new globalizing syntheses.

Table 3.1 presents the foregoing formulation in diagrammatic form. Here the conception of globalization and localization is indicated in the columns. That each interactively impacts on the other across a short time frame is depicted by the two horizontal arrows, whereas the single arrow that is segmented by stages highlights the presumption that globalization is the driving force of history and the basis of a dialectical process. In other words, rather than being merely a sum of diverse outcomes, a complex of dependent variables, the dialectic is a causal force unto itself, a convergence of independent variables that, taken together, sustain and expand the globalizing and localizing tensions which get reported in each day's headlines.

To theorize that the dialectical process fostered by the dynamics of globalization and localization has long been part of the human condition is not, of course, to imply that its functioning is readily discernible. On the contrary, springing as it does from underlying processes that may or may not be manifest at all times, its consequences were obscured in the twentieth century by world wars and the Cold War (which focused attention on national concerns) and in earlier centuries by the slower pace at which life unfolded (thus making globalizing and localizing events seem independent of each other). But today, with the superpower rivalry over and with a wide array of technologies quickening the pace at which people and communities are becoming ever more interdependent, the power created by the joining of globalizing and localizing dynamics, the tensions they foster, and the dialectical process they may generate are greatly enhanced and increasingly manifest. Indeed, there has been a veritable ground swell of articles and books which, in one way or another, take note of the tensions and posit them as relevant to the particular problems of concern to their authors.[4] Largely missing from this burgeoning literature, however, are attempts to probe the dialectical process itself, to explore its sources and anticipate its potential ramifications for ever wider realms of human experience.[5]

As a coherent process that is continually unfolding with inordinate speed in contradictory directions, the dialectic cries out for a label. Some years ago I tried to formulate the problem in more abstract terms so that it could be recognized as operative at every level of human organization – local and domestic as well as international – and in every realm of human endeavour – social and economic as well as political. In order to emphasize both the interactive and all-pervasive nature of the problem I coined a single word which was designed to irritate and thus linger. Unfortunately, it was so irritating that it was quickly dismissed. Yet, the course of events in the last decade have so richly and amply surfaced the problem that I dare to propose the word again. It is 'fragmegration,' by which I mean to suggest that the dynamics of fragmentation and integration at work in the world are woven together into a single interactive process.[6] As such, as a symbol of the interconnectedness of seemingly contrary patterns, of distant proximities, my irritating label may be theoretically more important than it appears. 'Fragmegration' suggests that the forces of centralization and decentralization can be a unified whole, a causal web in which they are simultaneously functions of each other.

Let me whet your appetite for this venture into theorizing about the causal web by suggesting that, if one is attuned to discerning the powerful forces unleashed by fragmegration, they are readily and widely evident. Examples of fragmegration abound. It can be easily seen in the former Soviet Union today, in the former Yugoslavia, in the Danish and French plebiscites on European Union, in the debates over the North American Free Trade Agreement, in the current controversy in the USA over what is politically correct, in the vast migrations of peoples, in the troubled conflicts of the Middle East, in the Los Angeles riot, in the racism in Germany that accompanied the large-scale influx of immigrants and that, in turn, provoked other Germans into holding candlelight marches in support of an open society,[7] in the tensions created in local American communities over unemployment resulting from the transfer of manufacturing operations abroad,[8] in the domestic turmoil generated in autocratic regimes by the emergence of global norms pertaining to human rights, and so on across virtually all the major issues that crowd the agendas of local, national and international systems. Perhaps the most succinct example of all is provided by the observation of Paul Friggerio, a leader of the Northern League that recently established itself as a regional party in Italy by recording considerable success in municipal elections: 'We care about being Lombards first and Europeans second. Italy means nothing to us."[9]

Yet it is one thing to recognize the causal web and quite another to frame theory that identifies when and how the two sets of dynamics play off each other. The theoretical challenge is enormous: How is the causal web established? How are the globalizing and localizing dynamics likely to undergo transformation as they re-shape each other? What joins the centralizing and decentralizing tendencies as a dialectical process? If globalization is the thesis and localization the antithesis, what gives rise to a synthesis? And keeping the continuous but staged arrow of Table 3.1 in mind, what transforms each synthesis into a new thesis that sends the dialectical process into another sequence? And how can we get a theoretical handle on phenomena that are constantly changing because the boundaries of distant proximities are being continuously redrawn?

Forms of Citizenship and Stimuli for Change

While a full-scale effort to develop theoretical clarity on these questions still lies ahead, let me try to make the case for such theory by indicating why the achievement of clarity is at the same time exciting, difficult and feasible. It is exciting because the task is to unravel the paradox of distant proximities. It is difficult because we have identified a complex problem pervaded by variability. Unlike realists, who proceed from the premiss that only states are key actors on the world stage and that all states proceed from the same essential motives, namely to maximize their own interests, we see the stage as peopled by a wide range of key actors in addition to states and we allow for the likelihood that they proceed from a multiplicity of contradictory motives. We perceive ethnic minorities, multinational corporations, subgovernments, social movements, concerned citizens, states, and a host of other actors who are all involved in the distant economic, social and political processes of globalization even as they seek to enhance the comfort and satis-factions of their close-at-hand family, group and community ties.

Nonetheless, despite the complexities and variabilities that do not lend themselves readily to elegant and parsimonious theory, the achievement of clarity seems feasible because it is possible to zero in on those points where the dialectical process is most intense, where the fragmegrative tendencies toward globalization and localization clash and thus necessitate the making of choices by individuals and organizations. My strategy for beginning to construct a theory of the dialectical process starts at the micro-level of individual citizens and their orientations toward fragmegrative dynamics. I would begin at this level not out of an idealism which posits citizens as exercising control over their own destinies, but because it is in individuals that the clash between globalizing and localizing tendencies originates and is most volatile. It is people who aspire to the security and order which come with centralization and to the immediate benefits and psychic comfort that comes with decentralization. It is people who welcome, contest, or otherwise experience the gains and losses that accompany revised conceptions of territoriality, transformed jurisdictions, shifting market shares, and changing cultural norms.

The power generated by these clashes is sustained by macro-organizations and institutions, and often the leaders of the macro-organizations and institutions can mobilize support for some form of synthesis between globalizing and localizing arrangements; but no amount of creative leadership at the macro-level is going to be effective unless people at the micro-level are responsive. It is the volatility of individuals which ultimately determines whether tensions between centralizing and decentralizing dynamics will flare and accelerate the dialectics of fragmegration.

It follows that if we can identify several alternative responses of individuals to a rapidly changing world, we can begin to evolve propositions about the sources and consequences of fragmegration. More accurately, if we can anticipate a range of systematic shifts in the responses of individuals that are linked to corresponding changes in the course of world affairs, we will be in a position to probe some of the circumstances under which the dynamics of globalization foster those of localization. An obvious theoretical strategy suggests itself: first, we need to differentiate prototypical ways in which people respond to their worlds; and, second, we need to identify developments in their worlds that can serve as stimuli to change. This is accomplished here by a four-way typology of individuals and by a less systematic identification of nine change stimuli.

The method used to differentiate among types of people involves what I call their *self-environment orientations*. The core hypothesis underlying the analysis is simple: to the extent that major shifts occur in the distribution of individuals among the four types of orientations, so will traces of these shifts be manifest in the institutions and policies of macro-collectivities and their relationships. Indeed, since the perspective and conduct of individuals at the micro-level is normally constant, the core hypothesis anticipates that the more the self-environment orientations of citizens around the world undergo transformation, the more intense will be the dialectical processes of fragmegration.

By self-environment orientations is meant the appraisal people make of the relative worth of themselves and their most relevant macro-collectivities. With globalizing and localizing dynamics undermining loyalties, shifting boundaries and proliferating organizations, a variety of collectivities – for example, societies, states, social movements, ethnic minorities, and transnational organizations – are candidates for greatest relevance. For purposes of simplicity here, I shall lump all such entities under the general heading of 'most salient macro-collectivity' – a term which allows for the possibility that a major redistribution of self-environment orientations may occur when the course of events leads to the formation of new collectivities or the collapse of old ones – and begin the analysis by treating the national society as the most salient collectivity toward which its members, citizens, maintain self-environment orientations.

As can be seen in Table 3.2, by dichotomizing between high and low appraisals of both self and society, four distinct types of citizens can be identified. Those who are inclined to treat their own needs as far more important than those of society practise what can be called *self-centred* citizenship. Persons who have the opposite tendency and place society's needs well ahead of their

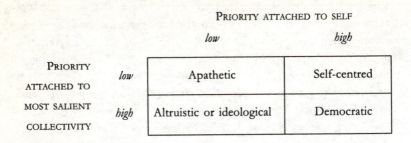

Table 3.2   Four Types of Citizenship

own practise either of two forms of citizenship: those who have an incremental approach to societal problems practise *altruistic* citizenship, whereas those who proceed from an inflexible image of what societal life ought to be practise *ideological* citizenship. People who are sceptical about the responsiveness of macro-politics to micro-inputs, or for other reasons attach little political significance either to their own or society's needs and are thus disinclined to enter the public arena, practise what can be regarded as *apathetic* citizenship. Finally, individuals who are deeply invested in the realization of both their own and society's needs are likely to practise a *democratic* form of citizenship. This balanced form approaches the democratic ideal in the sense that citizens are not unmindful of their own interests even as they recognize the necessity of also accommodating to the processes and goals of the larger collectivities to which they belong.

Elsewhere I have explored the current state of each of these four types of citizens; and, in so doing, I came to the clear-cut conclusion that the ever greater complexity of global life late in the twentieth century has had major consequences for the way in which people everywhere balance their own needs off against those of their larger societies.[10] With subnational groups becoming more salient as a result of localizing dynamics, and with transnational entities acquiring greater salience as a consequence of globalizing dynamics, most citizens at every point on the self-environment continuum are in motion, either searching for a new balance or struggling to reaffirm the old one. Like their ships of state, the anchors that tie citizens to core values have become unhooked, leaving their commitments adrift and their sails buffeted by cross-cutting winds. The inner need to maintain macro-attachments and political identities persists, but the foci of the attachments and identities have been increasingly obscured by transformative events. There are no moorings on to which people can readily latch.

If it is the case, therefore, that the world's publics are restless and that this micro-restlessness can have discernible macro-consequences, we can now turn briefly to the central theoretical question of how the fragmegrative dynamics of global politics might be affected by large-scale shifts in the several self-environment orientations. The key to this question is to be found in the diverse stimuli that can transform the balance between the priorities people attach to themselves and their most salient macro-collectivities. While self-environment orientations normally evolve for long stretches of time, both they and the identity of their salient collectivities are subject to change as the dialectics of globalization alter the relationship people establish with the political arena.

To theorize about the changes that can result in new self-environment orientations it is sufficient to note several change stimuli that can foster large-scale shifts in the conceptions people have of themselves and still others that can lead to large-scale redefinitions of their most salient collectivities. Any individual, of course, can be jolted into new self-environment orientations as a consequence of personal and idiosyncratic experiences; but here our theoretical concerns are confined exclusively to those stimuli that are likely to impact systematically on the self-environment orientations of large numbers of people.

Nine such change stimuli, all of them inextricably woven into the processes of globalization and localization, can be readily identified. One can be traced to the dynamism of information technologies, new educational opportunities, and a host of other factors that can enlarge the analytic skills people bring to the public arena and thereby increase their sense of connection to the course of events.[11] A second involves economic booms and busts that can raise or lower the confidence people have in their ability to cope with the turbulent dynamics of a changing world. A third set encompasses events in the public sphere – such as successful protests that topple governments – that serve to demonstrate the important role individuals may play in collective actions which bring about significant political realignments. A fourth set consists of corruption, policy blunders, decisional paralysis, and other forms of failure on the part of governments that can heighten the cynicism of publics or otherwise intensify their belief that nothing can be done to alleviate society's underlying problems. Fifth, a veritable explosion in the world's population of states and nongovernmental organizations has resulted in people having more and more collectivities to which they can attach salience.[12] Sixth, localizing dynamics have fostered an explosive subgroupism – a readiness of people to feel strongly about the more close at hand groups with which they are affiliated – that has served to reorganize their notions of what collectivities in the environment are worthy of their loyalties and concerns. Seventh, collectivities can experience spectacular triumphs or defeats in their interactions with other collectivities, and such outcomes can heighten the salience of the victors or lower that of the losers. Eighth, unexpected circumstances in the environment – such as the discovery of an ozone gap – can lead more and more people to join a social movement, and the momentum of the latter can sharpen its salience relative to other long-established collectivities. Lastly, dramatic events within a collectivity, such as a severe authority crisis or rampant inflation, can alter its esteem among its members and thus contribute to a systematic diminution of its salience.

In sum, the self-environment orientations of people are presently vulnerable to a number of challenges that can lead them to abandon their existing form of citizenship and take up a new form. Viewed in this way, the immediate theoretical question becomes that of estimating how major redistributions in the self-environment orientations of people might stem from the change stimuli and thereby sustain the fragmegrative dialectic.

The task is not as difficult as it might seem: since all of the foregoing change stimuli are presently agitated on a global scale, it is plausible to anticipate several paths along which fragmegrative dynamics can contribute to the redistribution of citizens among the types specified in Table 3.2. More specifically, four combinations of the above stimuli seem likely to sustain, if not to intensify, the dialectics of fragmegration. One combination – what might be called the 'authoritarian' dialectic – involves a severe authority crisis, a prolonged economic downturn, and a publicized record of recurrent corruption on the part of high-level governmental and other elites, circumstances that can result in systematic shifts toward apathetic or alienated self-environment orientations that are on a scale large enough to encourage demagogues to take advantage of the public's malaise, seize power, and undertake authoritarian rule at home and confrontation abroad. Second, if a well-documented deterioration of the natural environment occurs and energizes nongovernmental organizations even as it also highlights problems that governments alone cannot resolve, the combined impact of these developments along with the continuing spread of the skill revolution – what might be labelled the 'transnational' dialectic – can give rise to a wholesale shift toward altruistic self-environment orientations that lessen the salience of national governments and increase the salience of the environmental movement, thereby hastening the processes whereby authority is relocated in transnational directions. Third, sharp turns in the global economy, accelerated tendencies toward subgroupism, persistent stalemates within some or most of the world's major governments, and a proliferation of nongovernmental organizations that reach out to counterparts abroad for help in addressing their problems can combine – the 'individualizing' dialectic – to foster a systematic shift toward self-centred orientations that further paralyse governments and encourage people to define their interests as best served in a global or local rather than a national context. Finally, if the global economy grows at a steady rate, if authoritarian regimes are dramatically toppled by resolute citizens either in voting booths or the streets,[13] and if authoritarian regimes persistently demonstrate a readiness to heed as well as hear the demands of subgroups, the combined momentum of these developments – the 'democratic' dialectic – can generate a worldwide surge in appreciation of the delicate self-environment orientations that sustain democratic citizenship and thereby enable governments to break out of their stalemates and cooperatively address both the domestic and international problems currently dominant on the global agenda.

Since these four dialectical scenarios portend very different consequences for world politics, the question immediately arises as to which is the most likely to unfold in the years ahead. The answer seems obvious: all of them will probably evolve in different parts of the world. The adjustment to distant proximities need not be uniform. Given the transforming dynamics of fragmegration that have uprooted traditional ties and predisposed people everywhere into reworking the balance between their macro-attachments and their sense of political identity, the advent of different combinations of change stimuli is perfectly consistent with the diversity of prevailing conditions in the various regions and countries of the world. Indeed, since the globalizing and localizing dynamics are worldwide in scope, it is even probable that more than one of the dialectics will unfold within the same region and country. If this is so – if the future is likely to be marked by large-scale, simultaneous and interactive shifts in self-environment orientations on the part of ever more skilful publics – the present-day complexity of world affairs suggested by the metaphoric juxtaposition of the two photographs seems bound to endure well into the next century. And a long-term persistence of this complexity may well be desirable. Since two of the dialectics – those involving a predominance of self-centred or alienated citizens – are essentially noxious, it could well be argued that however intense continued fragmegration may be, it is the least risky equilibrium.

Conclusion

Let me end on a note of humility. While the analysis I have advanced here makes clear that the course of events is bound to be affected by the stirrings and demands that are currently at work in the homes and jobs of people everywhere, clearly I have not come even close to a specification of the dialectics of fragmegration. Much remains to be done and probably no single observer can accomplish the full task. Yet, the apparent relevance of the several dialectics identified here suggests that probing the relationships outlined in Table 3.1 may lead to a large theoretical payoff.

Notes

1. The original version of this chapter was delivered as the Morgan Lecture, Dickenson College, 27 October 1993. Revised editions were presented at the Annual Meeting of the International Studies Association (Washington DC, 30 March 1994) and at the College of William and Mary (Williamsberg, 12 April 1994). I am grateful to Hongying Wang for a number of insightful reactions to earlier drafts.

2. Joseph A. Camilleri, 'Rethinking Sovereignty in a Shrinking, Fragmented World', in R.B.J. Walker and Saul H. Mendlovitz, eds, *Contending Sovereignties: Redefining Political Community*, Lynne Rienner, Boulder, Colo. 1990, p. 29. For cogent assessments of the tensions between global and local concerns, see the various essays in Antoni Kuklinski, ed., *Globality versus Locality*, University of Warsaw, Warsaw 1990.

3. For further elaborations of these distinctions, see James N. Rosenau, 'The Person, The Household, The Community, and The Globe: Notes for a Theory of Multilateralism in a Turbulent World', paper presented at the UNU Symposium on Theoretical Perspectives on Multilateralism and Images of World Order (European University Institute, Florence, September 1992), and 'The Processes of Globalization: Substantive Spillovers, Elusive Exchanges, and Subtle Symbols', paper presented at the 60th Congress de l'Association Canadienne–Française pour l'Advancement des Sciences (Montreal, 13 May 1992).

4. See, for example, Zbigniew Brzezinski, *Out of Control: Global Turmoil on the Eve of the Twenty First-Century*, Charles Scribner's Sons, New York 1993; Samuel P. Huntington, 'The Clash of Civilizations?' *Foreign Affairs*, vol. 72 (Summer 1993), pp. 22–49; Kenneth Jowitt, *New World Disorder: The Leninist Extinction*, University of California Press, Berkeley 1992; Joel Kotkin, *Tribes: How Race, Religion and Identity Determine Success in the New Global Economy*, Random House, New York 1993; Antoni Kuklinski, ed., *Globality versus Locality*; Institute of Space Economy, University of Warsaw, Warsaw 1990; Ronnie D. Lipschutz, 'Reconstructing World Politics: The Emergence of Global Civil Society', *Millennium*, vol. 21 (Winter 1992), pp. 389–420; Zdravko Mlinar, ed., *Globalization and Territorial Identities*, Avebury, Aldershot 1992; and Max Singer and Aaron Wildavsky, *The Real World Order: Zones of Peace/Zones of Turmoil*, Chatham House Publishers, Chatham, N.J., 1993.

5. Noteworthy exceptions are Joseph A. Camilleri and Jim Falk, *The End of Sovereignty? The Politics of a Shrinking and Fragmenting World*, Edward

Elgar, Aldershot 1992; and Michael Zurn, 'Globalization and Individualization as Challenge for World Politics', paper presented at the 34th Annual Convention of the International Studies Association, Acapulco, Mexico, 23–27 March 1993).

6. James N. Rosenau, '"Fragmegrated" Challenges to National Security', in Terry L. Heyns, ed., *Understanding U.S. Strategy: A Reader*, National Defense University, Washington, DC 1983, pp. 65–82.

7. Stephen Kinzer, 'Germany Ablaze: It's Candlelight, Not Firebombs', *New York Times*, 13 January 1993, p. A4.

8. See, for instance, Steve Lohr, 'New Appeals to Pocketbook Patriots', *New York Times*, 23 January 1993, p. 37.

9. Quoted in Frank Viviano, 'Separatist Party on the Rise in Italy', *San Francisco Chronicle*, 3 March 1993, p. 1.

10. James N. Rosenau, 'Restless Publics as Sources of Global Turbulence', paper presented at the Table-Ronde on Individuals in World Politics, Congress of the Association Française de Science Politique, Paris, 24 September 1992.

11. For an extensive analysis of the impact of the skill revolution, see James N. Rosenau, *Turbulence in World Politics: A Theory of Change and Continuity*, Princeton University Press, Princeton, N.J. 1990, ch. 13.

12. James N. Rosenau, 'Organizational Proliferation in a Changing World', paper prepared for the Working Group of the Commission on Global Governance, May 1993.

13. Discussions of change generated in voting booths and on the streets can be found in James N. Rosenau and Michael Fagen, 'Domestic Elections as International Events', paper presented at the Conference on Collective Responses to Regional Problems: The Case of Latin America and the Caribbean, sponsored by the Carter Center and the American Academy of Arts and Sciences, Atlanta, 20 September 1993; and James N. Rosenau, 'The Relocation of Authority in a Shrinking World: From Tiananmen Square in Beijing to the Soccer Stadium in Soweto via Parliament Square in Budapest and Wenceslas Square in Prague', *Comparative Politics*, vol. 24 (April 1992), pp. 253–72.

4

Theorizing the Interregnum: The Double Movement and Global Politics in the 1990s

Stephen Gill

Writing from the prison where he was incarcerated by the Italian fascists, Antonio Gramsci (1971) summarized the world-order situation of the 1920s and 1930s in the context of the emergence of Fascism, Nazism and militarism, economic depression and rival politico-economic spheres of influence. The world order was in a process of structural transformation from an old order to a new. As Gramsci (1971) put it, 'The old is dying, the new is being born, and in the interregnum there are many morbid symptoms.'

In this chapter, then, the term 'world order' is not equated with stability: rather, it simply conveys a recurrent pattern of social forces and structures over time, as in the interwar order which was highly unstable, violent, and led to the outbreak of a total and brutal war. Philosophers, scientists and poets alike have claimed that the 1930s and 1940s represented a global civilizational crisis, even greater in scope than that which led to the outbreak of World War I. Thus the interwar order (1919–39) was unstable and non-hegemonic in quality. By this I do not mean hegemony defined in the realist sense of the dominance of one state over others. Rather, I use a √ Gramscian conception: here hegemony would be equated with the foundation and establishment of a system with relatively universal appeal, with mechanisms which permit the institutionalization of conflict and the weighting of subordinate interests in a transnational political settlement – a situation which was approximated, at least in the OECD regions, during the 1950s and 1960s, albeit in the context of the Cold War.

Since the early 1970s, however, the world has become more unstable; and with the collapse of communism we can now see a resurgence of deeply reactionary forces in many countries, as social inequality intensifies. This means that for a majority of people on the planet the future appears to be bleak – and, for the young, life will be worse than that experienced by their parents. Indeed, if many present trends continue (and are not politically countervailed), for many the world might come to resemble the one depicted metaphorically by Goya in his painting *Saturn devouring [one of] his children*: an allegory of the decay and ultimate destruction of civilization – and its collective future – through wantonness and violence.[1] Goya's macabre image might, at first glance, appear to some to be a rather pessimistic way to represent the possibilities for world order in the 1990s and beyond, although it seems apt given that many of the victims of world society are women and children, especially in the Third World. Nonetheless, I would wish to follow again one of Gramsci's favourite political maxims, which he drew from Romain Rolland: 'pessimism of the intelligence, optimism of the will' (Gramsci, 1971).

Pessimism here does not mean determinism. Nor does it imply that there is no scope for human agency and social choice, even for those who appear to be the most powerless. Our analysis should be concerned with structural change and with the question of human agency. In the 1990s, the image of Saturn might better refer to the relentless thrust of capital on a global scale, a thrust which has broken some of its previous terrestrial shackles. The growth in this global power has been accompanied by a neo-liberal, *laissez faire* discourse which accords the pursuit of profit something akin to the status of the quest for the holy grail; and the agencies associated with this discourse are staffed by neo-classical economists who assume – in matters of social policy – the role of a modern priesthood. Deviation from their orthodoxy is viewed as a sign of either madness or heresy, a view which acts to disarm criticism and to subvert the development of alternatives.

Nevertheless, one might argue that what is emerging in world politics in the 1990s is something akin to the 'double movement' outlined by Karl Polanyi in *The Great Transformation* (1957). By this

Polanyi – in some ways reminiscent of Gramsci – referred to the historical countermovements which attempted, in disparate but interrelated ways, to reassert social control over the movement towards the unfettered power of capital in determining the possibilities for social choice. Polanyi's two cases of this were in the late nineteenth century, and again in the interwar period, after the attempts to restore a liberal world economic order under Anglo-American dominance in the 1920s. Today we can relate the metaphor of the 'double movement' to those sociopolitical forces which wish to assert more democratic control over political life, and to harness the productive aspects of world society to achieve broad social purposes on an inclusionary basis, across and within different types of civilization. This involves a critique of the moral bankruptcy and social consequences of the narrow application of a crass consumerist materialism which lies at the heart of the neoliberal discourse.

With these highly political issues in mind, the purpose of this chapter is to sketch a historical materialist conceptualization of selected aspects of the political economy of the emerging world order, so as to probe its limits and contradictions. In normative terms, my purpose is to develop a form of understanding which can contribute to the construction of alternatives to the present world-order configuration, one based upon the principles of democratization and diffusion of power, greater social equity and human autonomy, moderation, and where possible non-violence in dealing with conflict. All of this means collective action – at local and global levels. This is necessary to countervail repressive, morbid and dehumanizing forces (for example, the orthodox deflationary policies of the *rentier* liberals on the one hand, and the forces of authoritarianism and fascism on the other) in the emerging world order.

Conceptualizing World Orders

To make sense of the vast complexity of the emerging world order, our conceptualization should involve the social forces of ideas (including ideologies, ethics, intersubjective meanings), institutions (such as state, and market, international organizations) as well as material aspects of social life (production broadly defined, including the means of destruction). We need to analyse the nature of this order at the levels of production, state and civil society, and world order (Cox, 1987). We need to do so with a sense of responsibility and thus combine political economy and ethico-political analysis. We can then analyse changes in world order in terms of the dialectic between forms of state, structures of production and ethico-political life. This requires an integrated form of political economy analysis which is open to conceptual and theoretical innovation. In this chapter, 'order' is understood as how things actually are, in a particular historical period, not as a normatively desirable or stable condition. To synthesize both Cox (1987) and Braudel (1981), a world order consists of a relatively persistent pattern of ideas, institutions and material forces which form historical structures over time, where structures can transcend particular societies or civilizational forms, in both space and time. Historical structures and the nature of political consciousness together configure the 'limits of the possible' for different groups, classes and nations.

The type of structural analysis I have in mind draws on the idea of historical structures, or patterns of behaviour which take on a particular character over time. Collective actions of human beings form historical structures with particular temporal duration. Since these structures are historically specific they cannot be adequately explained by using transhistorical generalizations, such as those associated with cyclical theories of history (for example, those which theorize the rise and decline of nations, hegemonies and empires). Rather, social scientific innovation is related to a 'second-order reality' which is not fully knowable (it involves the consciousness and intersubjectivities of human beings who can change the course of their actions). Thus social scientific generalizations must be limited and require a conditional vocabulary (Gunnell, 1968). At the same time, human action can change these structures. One should seek to analyse clearly the realities of our current situation. In this context we should outline the nature of, and potential for changes in, the 'limits of the possible' (Braudel, 1981). This is especially important for those groups who seek to democratize and to humanize global society. This is the essence of scholarly responsibility and it corresponds to the notion of 'critical political economy' outlined by Robert Cox in this volume (Chapter 2). Intellectual pessimism links to the hope and the expectation that such analysis might serve in a small way to help form a collective political will. Thus the first task is to analyse recent historical developments and their implications for different human collectivities.

Since the 1970s, there has been a shift towards a neo-liberal, disciplinary world order, although this is now in the process of being countervailed and constrained. I will discuss this in more detail later. One aspect of neo-liberal dominance is the growing structural power of capital, relative to labour, and relative to states. This neo-liberal shift involves, then, the growing strength and positional power of neo-liberal ideas (for example, my comments about heresy and the economics priesthood, above), their application in the practices and organizational forms of key social institutions (for example, state, market, international organization), and the reconfiguration of material power relations and a redistribution of wealth (with the growth in the power of capital, relative to labour). Instead of discipline being exercised authoritatively (for example, through social institutions such as the state, the family, churches), increasingly this discipline is market-based, and both direct (for example, capital's superior bargaining power over labour, or relative to states which bid for investment against one another) and indirect (for example, discipline exercised on firms, their workers, or on governments in the financial – especially stock and bond – markets). At the same time, the trends of the 1970s have gone with a deterioration in the material position of women, especially in the Third World and the former communist states.

Of course, there are many differences between the interwar period and the 1990s. Much of the world in the 1990s experiences what can be called – for want of a better expression – a form of not only market discipline, but of organized chaos (Vieille, 1988). By this I mean it is systematic in form, linked to the spread of *laissez faire* ideas and practices, and is sustained politically by a relatively affluent, politically active minority of the world's population (this minority is larger than that in the 1930s, partly because of the widening of political participation and economic growth). It is chaotic in the sense that the integration of the world into a single market also involves the disintegration of existing sets of social arrangements and state forms – such that social provision of many basic public goods becomes unsustainable. Most fundamentally, such organized and institutionalized chaos stems from the increasingly liberalized economic structures of contemporary capitalism. Often this chaos worsens because of the actions of instrumental, irresponsible, unaccountable or corrupt political elites or ruling classes. In this context, a relentless social Darwinism is tending to increase the level of socioeconomic inequality and political marginalization in much of the world, and, dialectically, to generate a growing disillusion with conventional organized politics.

Whilst a minority of the world's population enjoys relatively affluent and secure conditions in 'islands' of 'contentment', a substantial proportion of the world's population lives in vast 'seas' of poverty, and in situations characterized by insecurity, economic deprivation, ecological degradation and violence. The maxim of distributive justice of this system, to paraphrase the Book of Matthew is, 'to him that hath shall be given, from him that hath not shall be taken away'. Thus, although one could argue that the recent extension and deepening of the power of capital is equivalent to the latest phase of the bourgeois revolution, we are witnessing more generally a crisis of development of global proportions. Indeed, there is a revolution of the powerful against the weak. Nevertheless, the powerful are not omnipotent, and it is possible to speak of the power of the powerless, in the sense of the everyday forms of resistance to oppression and to commodification of life (Scott, 1993). At the same time, the failure of political orthodoxies in the context of economic depression and the collapse of communism are giving rise to new forms of right-wing authoritarianism and fascism.

In other words, since the onset of global economic crisis in the early 1970s, at least at the global level, a particular model of capitalist development – Anglo-American neo-liberalism – has tended to prevail. This model, in turn, is based on a set of institutions and practices which tend to promote a Social Darwinist reconfiguration of priorities, policies and outcomes. The most pervasive – and perverse – consequence of this shift has been a rapid deepening of social inequality within particular states and social formations, and between nations. It is reflected in the observations of many – from disillusioned former Thatcherites to religious and civic leaders, including the Pope – that capitalism has moved into a brutalizing and criminal phase, especially in parts of the Third World and the former Soviet Union. Bound up with this tendency is the intensification of (international) competition, and not only between firms. It involves also a competition between state forms, both in the sense of their ability to attract and retain flows of mobile capital and investment, and in terms of the appropriateness of their social structures of accumulation for social cohesion and economic growth – for example, the debate concerning competing capitalisms (Michel Albert's [1993] book on Anglo-American versus 'Rhineland' capitalisms, with its critique of the contradictions of the US obsession with short-term profit).

Thus, whilst neo-liberal discourse characterizes much Anglo-American thinking in matters of economics, and is practised in a variety of important contexts – for example, in the conditionality attached to loans from the World Bank and International Monetary Fund – different models of capitalist development characterize the political economies of East Asia and parts of Western Europe. Nevertheless, the Anglo-American neo-liberal model – and the social forces it seeks to promote and to protect – form the centrepiece of structural adjustment programmes for both the Third World and the former communist states.

A good example of the way that the conflicts in modern capitalism are mediated and synthesized politically is the GATT negotiations, which have been almost totally dominated by corporate interests (mainly from the G7 countries). The major thrust of the negotiations has been to reinforce the property rights and entry and exit options of transnational corporations. The agricultural negotiations have been conducted in ways which are designed to protect wealthy agribusiness interests in the richer countries, even though they have been the subject of intense conflicts between the

USA and the EC (Japan continues to protect its rice farmers for internal political reasons – they are key pillars of support for both conservative and social-democratic parties). Other examples of the way that the autonomy of even the most powerful states are subordinated to the interests of large capital and a *rentier* view of monetary policy are the EC 1992 and Maastricht initiatives, the latter of which is exemplary in so far as it proposes to tie the hands of future governments with regard to their freedom of :manoeuvre in monetary and fiscal policy. The NAFTA, if it is accepted by the US Congress, can also be seen as a vehicle to extend corporate power in North America, and, in the words of one of its supporters, the wealthy banker David Rockefeller, to 'politically lock in' neo-liberal reforms in Mexico, Canada and potentially in Chile. Politically, what is occurring is a process whereby new constitutional and treaty arrangements are put in place to institutionalize the privileges of capital on a world scale – and in so doing undermine the sovereignty and political autonomy of individual nation-states – and also macro-regional associations like the EC.

In this context, the Third World – in contrast to the movement for a New International Economic Order in the 1970s – has become increasingly fragmented, divided and weakened, so that it can no longer be regarded as an autonomous actor in global politics. Perhaps the notion of a united Third World was always more of a social myth than an attainable potential, given the diversity within and conflicts among states and social forces in Third World regions. However, this did not necessarily appear to be the case in the 1970s, in the era of OPEC and the NIEO. Since then, the threat of the countervailing power of OPEC to Western interests has been incorporated and, more significantly, diluted by the development of alternative sources of energy, thus undermining the market power of the Third World oil producers. Even here, the unity of apparently similar Third World nations – for example, the Arab oil producers – has more an element of fiction than of fact. The divisions within Islamic countries were reflected in the Iran–Iraq war of the 1980s, with Western interests, in turn, backing both sides, as the long war dragged on to a stalemate. The Gulf War of

1991 was the first 'post-Cold War' conflict for the USA (in the words of US Secretary of State, James Baker). This war attempted to reassert the supremacy of the US military and its role as guardian of the neo-liberal world order. In crushing Iraq, not only did the USA make it known that it intended to retain ultimate control over Middle Eastern oil supplies; it also conveyed the message that its military forces would act in future as global mercenaries, provided that (a) its key allies and clients (including Saudi Arabia) pay the necessary tribute, and (b) the US forces suffered minimal casualties.

US policing and surveillance power is linked, albeit indirectly, to social forces which serve to sustain internally neo-liberal policies in the Third World. Many of today's Third World leaders and administrators were trained in the West's universities in an era of conservatism, and in a period when *laissez faire* economics achieved something of the status of a holy doctrine. Many such individuals (for example, President Salinas of Mexico) have assumed high office in their own countries. Others have, or may have, worked as employees for the World Bank or IMF. Their 'domestic' constituency is affluent urban dwellers in the Third World. This explains why the international nexus of neo-liberalism has been associated with the rewarding of concessions and privileges to a very small stratum of the population. Affluent urban dwellers in the Third World – the counterpart to what J.K. Galbraith (1992) has called the 'culture of contentment' in the West – have been the primary beneficiaries of aid flows and World Bank loans. Most of the World Bank loans spent, for example, on infrastructure (water and electricity supply, ports, roads, urban transport) bypass the poor. A recent report, citing a typical case, showed that World Bank infrastructure subsidies in Bangladesh were six times as large to the rich as to the poor. Despite the investment of about US$200bn per year in developing countries, inefficiency, corruption and no maintenance of plant, machinery and infrastructure have meant that much of the money is wasted, and the poor – especially poor women and children – continue in their oppression and hunger.[2]

This scandalous state of affairs prompts me to remind the reader that we live in a world where approximately 800 million people live in the affluent parts of the world (not all are affluent: many are poor). A similar number of people are on the point of starvation in the Third World, where social inequality is massively more pronounced than in the privileged regions. In much of the Third World the 'four horsemen of the apocalypse' stalk the earth, in the form of war, violence, disease and epidemics (such as AIDS), and famine. For a large proportion of the world's population, conditions are often worse than those experienced by the urban and especially rural masses in the fifteenth to eighteenth centuries (Braudel, 1981), and all the evidence for the period since the late 1960s has shown that this situation is getting worse:

> Many governments fail today to enable their people to meet even their most basic needs. Over 1.3 billion lack access to safe drinking water; 880 million adults cannot read or write; 770 million have insufficient food for an active working life; and 800 million live in 'absolute poverty', lacking even rudimentary necessities. Each year 14 million children – about 10 per cent of the number born annually – die of hunger. (MacNeill et al., 1991: 6)

Nevertheless, I would suggest that such neo-liberal practices – in the context of others – may be ethically, politically, economically and ecologically unsustainable, in part because of a counter-mobilization to neo-liberalism, an issue I return to in the concluding part of the chapter.

Global Political Economy in the 1990s

Explaining the transition from a relatively integral and hegemonic order to a post-hegemonic one is complex and cannot be done here (on this, see Gill, 1990). Thus my explanation of the new forces and dynamics in the political economy of world order will necessarily be an oversimplified and schematic one because of constraints of space. However, an initial way to explain the developments in the 1980s is with reference to the restructuring and strengthening of the power of capital on a world scale, in the context of increased levels of competition and innovation (Gill and Law, 1989). In Toffler's phrase, the world became more clearly divided between the 'fast' and the 'slow' (Toffler, 1990). Toffler argues in effect that, inevitably, in the restructuring of the global political economy, the fast succeed and the slow fail or are marginalized. At the same time, in the deep recession of the early 1990s, many of the 'fast' went to the wall economically, destroying millions of businesses: a social Darwinism which afflicted the affluent as well as the poor.

Nevertheless, the global economy is dominated by, concentrated in, and organized from, a number of mega-sized urbanized regions or world cities (and their contiguous hinterlands) which form the major centres of production and consumption, and which house the vast bulk of corporate headquarters. These privileged 'islands' of production and consumption are organized hierarchically, and are both internally and externally policed and thus defended and protected from the encroachment of the marginalized people of world society.

Several elements in this complex process of the restructuring of the global may be highlighted. I start with the most general 'material forces', and then discuss new discourses of power and mutations in forms of state, and the intensified commodification of social relations. It is beyond the scope of a short chapter to discuss other aspects of the political economy of world order – for example, strategic realignments and militarization – crucial though they are.

The restructuring of production and finance

The restructuring of global production since the early 1970s (and the late 1960s in Japan as it turned to more information- and capital-intensive production) was intimately connected to both the onset of a third industrial–technological revolution and the growing power of transnational capital. This occurred in the context of greater international competition and intensified innovation in a period of slower growth, punctuated by recessions of increasing severity. Restructuring accelerated in the 1980s (especially during and following the 1979–82 recession, the most severe since the 1930s). These conditions entailed growing pressures on states and economic agents (individuals, firms, unions, governments), speeding up the necessary response time for economic (and political) survival.

There was an accelerating shift away from Fordism to post-Fordism in the OECD region. Fordism here denotes the system of accumulation based on mass production and mass consumption which originated in the USA in the 1920s and which spread globally in the post-World War II period. The auto and consumer electronics industries are exemplary here, in that both required semi-automated mass production and a mass market based upon rising real wages, in a demand-led system which was pump-primed by government policies. Economic policy was primarily Keynesian in complexion and reflected a great deal of confidence among economists and planners that the business cycle could be fine-tuned and that the scourge of capitalist depression had been finally eradicated. However, the conditions of the 1950s and 1960s were especially propitious for Keynesianism and Fordism, since surging demand was fuelled by postwar reconstruction, a regime of cheap energy, and a number of other conjunctural factors which all began to change by the early 1970s. At this time, production became less mass based, more specialized and 'flexible' (involving more part-time, often female, workers, and less security of employment for virtually all), and the golden age of postwar welfarism and corporatism – the political counterparts of Fordism – began to draw to an end.

In some senses much of the restructuring in the 1980s was 'ultra-Fordist': it entailed longer work hours, more control over labour, increased work intensity, increased use of machines, and so on), and an associated secular decline in the power of traditional forms of organized labour. Labour discipline tightened and increasing numbers of workers were subordinated more comprehensively in the workplace and the home to the rhythms and dictates of the new organizational systems and forms of surveillance.

National systems of financial regulation and control – a centrepiece of Keynesian planning and macroeconomic management – were displaced by an integrated, and much less regulated, 24-hour global financial system, which some commentators, following John Maynard Keynes's *General Theory* (1936), have suggested resembled a casino. A casino is in reality a structured environment where the gambling odds are significantly weighted in favour of the 'bank'.

Not only was the new global financial system outside the control of any single government (except perhaps that of the US); it operated systematically in favour of financial interests, as opposed to those associated with productive manufacturing or with government planning. Access to credit became organized not only on a global scale but also in a much more discriminatory and hierarchical manner, and in ways which emphasized the short-term over the longer-term. This meant a type of law of the jungle, with only the fittest able to survive. Other aspects of the Keynesian metaphor are significant. A short-term speculative mentality came to prevail in the relatively deregulated financial markets. Indeed, Susan Strange (1986), like Keynes in the 1930s, suggested that this type of development is inimical not only to production, but also to the ethico-political legitimacy of liberal democracy.

These developments, then, helped to give rise to a more competitive, social Darwinist struggle of the survival of the fittest, and a growth in social inequality within and between nations. Indeed, the already massive gap in income and wealth between the richest 10 per cent and the poorest 10 per cent of the people on the planet increased almost tenfold during the 1980s, according to United Nations statistics. Nevertheless, by the late 1980s economic globalization approached levels which approximated those immediately prior to 1914, often considered to be the high-water mark of capitalist economic internationalism. At the same time, it is important to remember that the areas and populations who are the beneficiaries of the global political economy still represent a small proportion of the world's population. In this context there is a simultaneous and interlinked process of incorporation and/or marginalization into/from the global political economy. This process can be illuminated with reference to the wrenching transitions – involving town and country, agriculture and industry – occurring in much of the Third World.

Those who are completely marginalized from the production and consumption aspects of the global political economy are, for example, subsistence farmers in Africa. However, many peasants are forced off the land and often go to the cities and may be incorporated into production for the global economy, such as the peasant women who work as cheap, 'dextrous and docile' workers in the factories in the Maquiladoras in Mexico. For the rest of the world, the processes of incorporation/marginalization which I have mentioned have continued, often with devastating consequences as in Africa and Latin America, where real incomes fell precipitately in the 1980s. These processes are, albeit in different ways, mirrored within the OECD countries, where a growing underclass is increasingly visible, even in wealthy societies with apparently low unemployment such as in Japan.

New constitutionalism and mutations in forms of state

In other essays (for example, Gill, 1992a and 1992b) I have linked the new discourses of power which have emerged in the OECD countries – in the context of the neo-conservative 'revolution' of the 1970s and 1980s – to the idea of a 'new constitutionalism'. This can be understood as a term intended to describe the varied and complex efforts, especially by the forces of the political right and those of neo-classical economists and financial capital, to develop a politico-legal framework for the reconstitution of capital on a world scale, and thus for the intensification of market forms of discipline. That is, one way to interpret the latest phase in the worldwide bourgeois revolution is in terms of a new level of global-ization of capitalist production and competition, with the need for institutional and political innovation as a counterpart – ideology is not enough to secure the property rights and political prerogatives of capital on a world scale.

This discourse serves to protect the privileges of the dominant agents in the new forms of oligopolistic competition in the 1980s, and to restrain future governments from intervening to undermine such privileges. This is also linked to attempts to privilege business and business-oriented ideas in parts of the public sector (which may be difficult to privatize, such as health care and education), whilst decreasing the accountability of parts of the public sector. Both of the above relate, then, to the broader purpose of extend-ing and deepening the power of capital, in both the 'public' and 'private' sectors.

The new constitutionalism seeks to reinforce a process whereby government policies are increasingly accountable to (international) capital, and thus to market forces (especially those exercised in and from the financial markets). Sovereignties, political associations and forms of state are redefined to reflect this new categorical imperative. State policies thus become more attuned to the imperatives of global economic forces, in the context of the new ideologies of competitiveness and 'human capital'. Increasingly governments in the OECD countries – and worldwide – seek to strengthen political discipline, in part to provide a more hospitable investment climate to attract production. Credibility with the financial markets is, for governments, becoming perhaps more important than credibility with voters.

The Maastricht agreements, for example, mandate strict limits on budget deficits at precisely a moment when fiscal expansion might help to alleviate a slump. However, the competitive aspect of the new constitutionalism impels political leaders to seek to outbid others in providing for a low-inflation investment climate (with the French attitude tantamount to stressing the need for a strong franc as a symbol of national virility). Another aspect of the 'new constitutionalism' is the idea of central bank independence, freeing monetary policy from direct political control, in ways which are, it is argued, beneficial for long-term price stability (zero inflation) *à la* Bundesbank. Such moves have continued in the 1990s, not only in eastern Europe, but worldwide. In the European case, the Maastricht agreements provide for the eventual development of an independent central-banking superstructure. Thus the situation resembles the 1930s in two ways: developments are seeking to reinforce the prerogatives of *rentier* capital, and in the sense of the pursuit of a politics of austerity in Europe (caused in part by the economic effects of German unification, which was badly mishandled by the Kohl government).

More broadly, the effect of such policies has been to undermine political support for European union, in so far as there is a competitive rather than cooperative solution to continental and global economic problems, and in that protracted economic slump is giving rise once again to right-wing political movements and a politics of atavism, disenchantment, anxiety and racism. In this way, the 'fast' and the 'strong' (Toffler, 1990) are increasingly sorted and (partly) protected from the 'slow', the weak and the under-privileged. Not only large numbers of individual workers, but also thousands of managers and business have been forced to the wall in the early 1990s – especially in Europe, where the economic situation was made worse by the deflationary policies associated with the totemic ERM.

It is in the context of this restructuring of production and political discourse and practice that we should locate recent changes in the form of state, understood as both cause and effect of the processes we are discussing. By form of state we have in mind the nature of the relationship between state and civil society. This relationship can be understood both 'locally' and 'globally'. The restructuring of global production and power appear to have begun to transform the basis of political authority, legitimacy and accountability away from the national towards the transnational and global levels, whilst simultaneously the internal aspects of accountability and authority are being reconfigured, at the same time as what I have called the 'terrain of contestability' in the politics of the OECD has shifted to the right since the 1970s.

Two key and interrelated elements which have served to drive these changes are, on the one hand, the persistent fiscal crisis of the state (local, regional and national), and on the other, changing structural pressures from global financial markets, such as the bond markets, which mandate significant constraints on state budgets and have tended to press increasingly for a politics of austerity and a cut-back in state provision of social and educational expenditures. In the 1970s, the looming fiscal crisis in Latin America (and indeed in some OECD countries) was postponed if not alleviated by heavy (overseas) borrowing. As interest rates rose in the 1980s, along with worsening terms of trade for Latin American exports, fiscal and debt crisis ensued. These developments emerged, then, in the context of the globalization of finance and a regime of historically unprecedented (and very high) real rates of interest in the 1980s. This – along with a number of other factors – exerted structural pressure on the nature and direction of 'adjustment' to the new conditions. The disciplinary power of mobile financial capital (in the bond markets for example: through pension funds, insurance companies and large wealth holders, which can switch assets from one investment jurisdiction to another very easily and rapidly) was supplemented by the direct pressure exerted by the governments of the Group of Seven (G7) and international financial institutions (IFIs). Let us now relate these developments to a preliminary assessment of the way state forms are changing or mutating in the new social Darwinist universe.

The 'local' level

The first of these changes involves a 'domestic' shift from the welfare-nationalist state, a state form which was redistributive and which constrained the inherent tendency in capitalist economies towards deepening social inequality, and which organized the authoritative (that is, non-market) provision of a wide range of public goods. This state form characterized many of the OECD countries after World War II (and allowed for substantial state capitalism, domestic protection and social-welfare provision). We can now see a movement towards the 'competition' state (premissed on relative success in the world market and on attracting mobile capital for investment and finance through, for example, competitive deregulation and tax breaks to foreign investors). In parts of the Third World, the counterpart to this change is a shift from various types of state capitalism towards variants of a neo-liberal form of state.

As Polanyi noted, in the case of Britain, the creation of a self-regulating market society was not only an unprecedented and revolutionary development, it was also premissed upon a strong state which was able to implement and enforce the measures which created the market society: '*laissez faire* itself was enforced by the state [and involved] an enormous increase in the administrative functions of the state, which was now endowed with a central bureaucracy able to fulfil the tasks set by the adherents of liberalism' (Polanyi, 1957: 139). Today, the trend (or at least the announced aim of liberal policy) is towards downsizing this bureaucracy and making its operations more 'economical' or efficient, and imbued with market values.

Nevertheless, despite attempts to roll back the scale of the state in the economy, developments in the OECD regions suggest that all that has been accomplished is a slowing down of the growth of the state apparatus – a growth which accelerated in the postwar era of welfare-nationalist capitalist development – and a steady growth in unemployment. Moreover, as I have noted, competing models of the appropriate state form for capitalism – including the social-market model of Germany (and Jacques Delors' European social-democratic model) and the state mercantilism of Japan – are competitors to Anglo-American *laissez faire* neo-liberalism, and part of their claim to superiority is often couched in terms of the greater social solidarity and longer-term time horizons they seek to promote.

However, the general trend has been towards a gradual universalization of the neo-liberal model and neo-liberal discourses concerning competitiveness and (market) efficiency. Whereas constitutional and legal arrangements have begun to redefine the relationship between state and civil society from a neo-liberal perspective, these developments are supplemented by new organizational and other innovations, backed by coercive as well as consensual mechanisms of power at the micro-level. Both macro- and micro-levels of power taken together help to explain the political form of disciplinary neo-liberalism. Both private and public forms of surveillance have intensified in the 1980s. Innovations in organization theory as well as developments in computers and associated network technologies have facilitated this.

Within governments, there has been a general shift in the pecking order of ministries, with finance ministries tending to become most important, and with those responsible for employment and social security subordinated to financial principles and methods of control imported from commercial life. One vehicle for this is the formation of quasi-governmental organizations (for example, British government 'quangos') which oversee parts of the public sector at the intermediate level (that is, below the ministerial level). Another, more far-reaching example is the restructuring of the public sector in New Zealand. Here, inspired by the ideas of the right-wing public-choice school (pioneered by James Buchanan and Gordon Tullock), Treasury officials developed a system whereby every government department has been forced to operate on business lines. Each department has a performance agreement with a minister, who explicitly 'purchases' policies on a contractual basis from the bureaucrats, with former permanent heads renamed as chief executives, now appointed on fixed-term contracts:

> Not every chief executive is thrilled by the new regime. It provides, after all, just the sort of targets, monitoring techniques, incentives and performance measures that prevail in the business world but are anathema to many public servants worldwide. But politicians of all stripes are beginning to recognize the system's potential to squeeze better value for every taxpayer dollar. (Mather, 1993)

Thus the new constitutionalism is matched by a process of (quasi-) privatization in the public sector, and a relative insulation of the public sector from the pressures of democratic accountability. Global financial capital draws much of its strength from the division of the globe into competing jurisdictions which can be played off to make arbitrage profits, and maximizes its power through minimizing any restrictions on its mobility or curtailment of property rights. By the same token, the division of ministries into units of financial control makes these institutions more amenable to marketization and the introduction of competition within as well as between ministries. The managers and workers of the state sector are led to behave as if they were marketplace animals.

Increasingly in the OECD countries the police, security services, tax and the health and welfare administrations have integrated database systems which enhance surveillance capabilities. The popular climate encouraging surveillance has gone with the vast increases in crime (especially crime against the person and vandalism) recorded in most OECD countries during the 1990s. Moreover, government agencies seek to obtain and to integrate private databases into their information structures as a matter of routine, for example to monitor the financial system and to pursue tax claims (for example, credit-rating and financial records). Another key motivation for this change is the drive to increase the effective rates of tax-collection as tax systems have been restructured away from direct taxation (for example, taxes on income, taxes on profits) towards indirect taxes (for example, sales and value-added taxes) at a time of fiscal crisis, and where the bond markets' willingness to buy government paper (to sustain provision of finance for budget deficits and for debt repayments) is in question.

Noteworthy here is that private agencies in various countries also have massive centralized databases, many of which contain public information (for example, the large bond-rating agencies, such as Standards and Poor), thereby indicating the difficulty of separating 'public' and 'private' aspects of surveillance and evaluation of market- and credit-risk. Thus, while governments are increasingly accountable to international market forces, this (external) accountability puts pressure on the bureaucracy and politicians to increase and deepen domestic forms of surveillance and social control in order to extract greater taxation from immobile firms and workers, in order to finance budget deficits. Thus a European Bank for Reconstruction and Development idea of using the Red Army as tax collectors (mooted in April 1993) can be related to the attempt by the authorities to eradicate crime and tax evasion and other forms unregulated economic activity in the informal or black economy. This type of development may be a harbinger of the future for the armies of indebted Third World countries, and for the reorientation of security and intelligence agencies worldwide.

The 'global' level

The second, 'global' dimension of changes in prevailing forms of state is a redefinition of external sovereignty and practice: a shift from the traditional mercantilist and developmental state towards more globalized neo-liberal state structures, consistent, for example, with IMF and World Bank structural adjustment programmes (SAPs). In this sense, the internal purposes and public goals of the state are increasingly subordinated to external (economic) considerations, and the domestic and the international are increasingly articulated through the interplay of international capital based on more global structures of production, finance and exchange.

Not all pressures were common to all states: for example, the USSR was pressured in large part because of its military-industrial rivalry with the USA and the West, and because its own system of production entered into crisis and absolute decline at a time when its legitimacy was increasingly brittle. Those states which failed to adapt to these new conditions either disappeared (for example, East Germany, the USSR) and/or began to disintegrate socially and economically (for example, many states in Africa, some in Latin America and some in eastern Europe).

Where adjustment occurred, and where the links to globalizing capitalism were maintained or extended, a restructuring of the state and a redefinition of the role of the state and the relationship between 'public' and 'private' took place. Gramsci's concept of the extended state (represented by the formula: state = political society + civil society) helps us to understand and to reconceptualize some aspects of this process. Political society includes the 'public' sphere of government, administration and law and order, as well as security. Civil society includes those elements normally considered 'private', such as free enterprise, political parties, Churches, trades unions, and so on. Centralized state structures and the forms of sovereignty associated with them are changing in ways which are more consistent with the development of a more market-driven form of civil society: statism and social protection are on the retreat and are giving way to a more individualistic, competitive and disciplinary political culture and society. Instead of the primary forms of discipline coming from the state, increasingly this regimen is market based, and is expressed most acutely in the sphere of finance.

The restructuring of state and capital on a world stage towards a more globally integrated and competitive market-driven system is the process we can call the 'globalization' of the state. It involves the transformation of the state so as to give greater freedom to the private aspects of capital accumulation in the extended state at the local, national and transnational levels. These changes involve the growth in the power of capital at both the 'domestic' and 'international' levels in a transnational process of class formation. In this sense, a key characteristic of global politics in the last decades of the twentieth century is a redefinition of the role and purpose of government in the emerging world order. This has been a transnational process, involving both key elements in the state structures of the most powerful members of the G7 (Canada, Britain, France, Germany, Italy, Japan, the USA and the EC) and drawn from private banks, corporations, think-tanks, universities, the media, and conservative and liberal political parties, as well as influential private international-relations councils such as the Trilateral Commission and the World Economic Forum. In Gramscian terms, this is a transnational historic bloc of forces (combining internationally oriented elements of the states and civil societies of many nations, but anchored in the leading positions of the G7 countries, especially the USA). We will, for the sake of shorthand, call this transnational historic bloc 'the G7 nexus'.

The 'G7 nexus' involves not only political society, or the state narrowly defined. It also involves dominant forces from within transnational civil society: for example, transnational firms and banks and international organizations. Thus the distinctions between 'public' and 'private' and 'domestic' and 'international' partly obscure the transnational nature of politics and the state within modern capitalism. Within this process, Kees van der Pijl (1989) argues that the 'Lockeian' state/civil society form has begun to spread and to supplant the more state-capitalist, centralized and regulated – or 'Hobbesian' – political economies. To a degree, politically centralized forms of capital accumulation are superseded by indirect, economic forms as the global political economy is restructured along neo-liberal lines. A global civil society, organized along Anglo-American Lockeian self-regulating principles increasingly becomes the primary model for emulation on a worldwide basis (with, as has been noted, European and East Asian variants as rivals). Seen in another way, the enlargement of the scope of the Lockeian state implies a worldwide shift towards what Polanyi (1957) termed a 'self-regulating' market form of society. This may – or may not – imply a corresponding constitutional form, premissed upon the separation of powers, the sanctity of private property, religious toleration and formal equality between the sexes.

Commodification and insecurity

Partly because of the developments noted above, the commodification of social relations within modern capitalism has deepened: this is a sociological counterpart to the growth in the power of capital relative to states and to labour. By commodification I mean the propensity of capitalist society to define and to quantify social life in market terms. Thus elements which were previously integrated into the fabric of society before the rise of modern capitalism now become subject increasingly to the laws of the marketplace. Thus land (nature), labour (lived time) and productive capacity (the construction of society, living space and the capacity to provide for human needs) become commodities which are bought and sold. Money becomes the principal medium of social exchange, and future production is in large part premissed upon the provision of credit, allocated in the capital markets.

Of course, this aspect of socioeconomic and cultural change in the 1980s has a long lineage. In this sense, the current phase of transformation – a deepening of commodification, especially since the early 1970s – can be related to Braudel's concept of *longue durée*. In this sense, the structure and language of social relations is more systematically conditioned by market forces and practices. This means that capitalist norms and practices increasingly pervade the *gestes répétés* of everyday life: in sports, in leisure, in play, in the process of consumption more generally. At the same time, the process of commodification is increasingly monitored, aggregated and controlled by the use of surveillance technologies. The process of consumption is massaged and channelled by mass communications, especially television. Privileged (that is, wealthier) consumers can be de-massified, according to market segments, and thus can be targeted more accurately. Potential consumers are identified and 'constructed', on the basis of very detailed and sophisticated information about their income, lifestyles, credit rating, health and criminal history, and so on. The use of these technologies is related to the spread of money and credit structures into more and more aspects of everyday life; that is, into not only the home, but also the workplace, such that in the USA it is increasingly difficult to obtain a job unless one has a good credit rating and health record. The basis for these information structures is to a large extent everyday transactional activity in the marketplace (Gandy, 1993).

In this context, there is a growing influence of what I call the 'new utilitarian' thinking. In the 1950s and 1960s the combination of welfare nationalism and the Fordist structures of mass production and mass consumption meant that capitalism in the OECD countries was both consumerist and socially inclusionary. Indeed, the phrase 'de-commodification' has been associated with the development of the welfare state in the Nordic countries, and in particular was reflected in the reforms associated with the so-called 'Swedish model' in the 1950s and 1960s. In today's OECD capitalism, we see a situation emerging which is both hyper-consumerist (and more commodified) and more socially exclusionary: higher unemployment and marginalization have meant that the more flexible forms of production have given rise to niche markets, whilst large numbers of people have insufficient income to enjoy more fully the fruits of production. Whereas in the 1950s and 1960s corporatist politics and the state steering of the economy through Keynesian policies meant that social choice was the product of relatively planned forms of capitalist development, in the 1980s and 1990s an increasingly narrow, utilitarian and short-term calculus appears to prevail.

More and more it seems that public policy is aimed at providing the greatest happiness to the greatest number of consumers – Jeremy Bentham's 'felicific calculus' – even though the privileges attendant on this may be more exclusive than before. One needs to be more specific here. The key group of consumers are those who are politically active, at least in the sense of voting in elections. In the USA this means, in typical presidential elections (where the turnout is highest) only about half of all eligible voters actually bother to vote, so that one can become a president with as little as 25 per cent of the potential vote. Those who do vote tend to be most attuned – at least in the USA – to maintaining the status quo, in the sense of the government policies which protect their position. Thus when I refer to the 'happiness' of the 'greatest number of consumers', I mean this not in the existential sense that each of these people is 'happy': merely that their social and economic situation is less unhappy and is better protected than that which pertains to the vast majority of the world's population.

The voting majority are thus provided for through the particular kinds of materialist consumerism which typify the 1990s – that is, through consumer goods and services, a quite narrow form of consumerism. As I have noted, the situation has been captured well in J.K. Galbraith's, *The Culture of Contentment* (1992), where perhaps half of the population in each OECD country is relatively contented with the state of things, whilst the general condition of the rest of the population deteriorates in relative (and in many cases, in absolute) terms. Moreover, the contented majority are supported by a system of protection and socialization of risk (for example, US legislation guaranteeing bank deposits up to a maximum of $100,000: by definition, the poor do not have such large savings). Many of its members in the USA openly support a large military, and they and their counterparts elsewhere often tend to be in favour of draconian forms of policing and punishment of offenders, harsh discipline for the ('working' and 'idle') poor, such as workfare, as well as ferociously opposing increased taxation of their own incomes. They favour policies which redistribute income upwards: towards the already wealthy or economically comfortable. They seek to sustain a situation where the law of the jungle operates for the rest of the world, with a system of social protection for themselves. In this sense, their outlook is short-sighted and me-oriented.

In this way the culture of contentment sanctions policies which directly or indirectly make the rest of the population worse off. An insidious counterpart to this development has been the so-called 'privatization' of security: that is, the preferential provision of personal security to those with the means to pay for it. For example, Galbraith points out that in the late 1980s there were more 'private' security agents or quasi-police than there were public law officers in the USA. Moreover, the housing complexes of the affluent (wherein resides a 'laager' mentality, according to Galbraith), as well as the suburban, up-market shopping malls in the USA, increasingly resemble fortresses, policed by armed guards, and monitored by video installations. These are designed not only to protect life and property, but, in the case of the shopping malls, to deter the 'wrong kind' of consumer from actually attempting to shop at the mall.

Another pernicious example of this process is the privatization of health care in the USA, with the effect that at least 30 million US citizens from a population of 254 million have no health care, and a similar number have coverage which is of limited quality. The sheer cost of this system (estimated at 14 per cent of the US GNP of over $4 trillion) has prompted the Clinton administration to make health-care reform its number-one domestic priority. It is worth emphasizing that two of the pillars of the postwar order in the bulk of the OECD countries were social guarantees of personal security and health care on an equal basis for all, and a consensus that the basic provision of these public goods should be taken out of the marketplace. It is not only in the USA that this consensus has been eroded significantly.

In addition, one reason why the 'felicity' of even well-paid workers in the OECD countries might be doubted is not just the rising levels of unemployment, a roll-back in work conditions and wages, and the precariousness of personal security as social disorder and crime increased in the 1980s and 1990s. Another is the intensification of discipline and surveillance in the workplace and the consumer society more generally. This creates anxiety, stress and depression among workers, including managers and middle-class professionals.

Organizational and technological innovations have entailed a shift towards flexible work practices, the intensification of work, longer hours and, at the same time, new forms of managerial, technological and social control; and are premissed upon the principle of the maximization of profit (or market share) and the avoidance of risk (managers are also placed under surveillance, both in the private sector, and in the public sector, as is shown in the example from New Zealand cited above) (see Gandy, 1993).

The new disciplinary structures of everyday life have also gone with attempts to strengthen state surveillance capacities, especially in matters relating to policing, taxation and social expenditures. As is indicated in the quotation from Mather above, a substantial motivation for this has been the fiscal crisis of the state, and the need to increase the effective rate of taxation to finance state programmes when interest rates remain high (especially when direct taxes have been cut in competitive tax-cutting in the 1980s).

One important question which this state of affairs raises is the degree to which this is, or can continue to be, a stable situation – economically, politically and socially. The growing lumpenproletariat and urban underclass which is to be found in almost all the major cities of the world may indicate that the numbers of 'happy' consumers may in fact be a shrinking minority, and that a situation of collective insecurity and longer working hours is intensifying at the personal or household level.

This raises the issue of a broad crisis of social reproduction and the long-term sustainability of the neo-liberal world order. This is seen at its most intense in the predicament of the vast majority of women in the Third World. Thus one aspect of the intensified commodification of everyday life which often goes unnoticed on the part of Western political economists is the way such commodification tends to operate, albeit indirectly, with a gender bias. Since many of the ultimate victims of this process are not only women but also children, it can be related to the social Darwinist tendencies outlined earlier, and gives a feminist twist to the theme of Saturn devouring *his* children.

As Beneria and Feldman (1992) illustrate, a range of studies of a variety of different Third World countries have shown that in almost all cases, structural adjustment programmes (SAPs) have had similar effects. Private capital shapes the process of reform, and this leads to cuts in health care, social welfare, education and public expenditure more generally, and the rapid creation of export-processing zones (for example, the Maquiladoras) and other means of shifting the economy from import substitution to export promotion. Other recent studies have shown that women's position has declined as they have become assimilated into neo-liberal capitalism; for example, land reform (producing larger landholdings for agribusiness such as that introduced in Mexico in preparation for the NAFTA) has undermined indigenous people's rights to common lands and forced peasants to sell their labour to the new landowners or to migrate to the cities in search of work (Tickner, 1991: 195–6). It might also be added that Third World women are crucial to dealing with global ecological problems since they tend to do most of the work on the land and gather most of the fuel (usually wood, and this is related to deforestation and the spread of deserts).

The export-led strategies and SAPs of the 1980s and 1990s have tended to fall disproportionately on women as providers of basic needs as social-welfare programmes in areas of health, nutrition and housing are cut. The result has been that the social cost of the reduction in public services has been forced back into the household, or down to the community level – and this usually means that women, especially Third World women, have an added burden to sustain. It has frequently been noted that women do approximately two-thirds of all the work in Third World societies – partly because they have responsibility for child rearing as well as for earning income in the labour market. The premiss of SAPs however, is that resource switching to internationally tradeable production is costless. Yet, as Diane Elson (1992) has argued, this is not true; and, indeed, even UNICEF's programme of 'adjustment with a human face' (a more compensatory version of the World Bank's prevailing view) indirectly accepts this. Whereas the UNICEF programme allows for the international dimension and the protection of the most vulnerable – for example, severe malnutrition of children, providing feeding programmes – it fails to recognize adequately that the switching of resources (that is, dumping the social costs into the households) means an extra and unequal burden for Third World women – or at least those outside the affluent urban enclaves (Elson, 1992: 30–31).

This is why many feminists have called for a new form of political economy with women's needs as its central, but not only, focus. Women's needs are seen as both 'practical' (involving the question of survival) and 'strategic' (involving changing the limits of the possible), and involve policies designed to transform both market and state. This is because often the state reinforces the situation of inequality between men and women through patriarchal family regulations, where women are treated as legal dependents of men. In this sense, women have a strategic interest in transforming the public sector, and in redefining the meaning of 'public' and 'private' in matters of political economy. With this in mind, proposals have been made for women in the public sector to develop coalitions with the women consumers of their services, and to use their collective power to press the importance of democratic politics. In addition, with regard to regulation of the market, these theorists point out that both the 'public' and the 'private' sectors need to be disaggregated, so that differential treatment can be accorded to large transnational corporations on the one hand, and to small, locally based (women's) cooperatives on the other (Elson, 1992: 39). At the same time, I would emphasize that it is important that the women's movement considers itself as part of a broader democratic and progressive movement.

The Contradictions of Neo-liberalism and Counterhegemony

The policies which have gone with new constitutionalist neo-liberal discourse are even queried by those interests which tend to benefit most from deflationary policies: financial and creditor interests more generally. This is because policies imbued with this type of orthodoxy have been globally deflationary, and have tended not only to accelerate the restructuring of production but also to increase mass unemployment and social unrest. In its most developed form, in western Europe, then, it is associated with protracted economic slump. Thus whereas politicians are able to press for deregulation and market discipline on grounds of greater efficiency, they do so in the context of what economists call the 'fallacy of composition': namely, if all deflate depression ensues. Moreover, politicians move towards new constitutionalist policies in ways which not only undermine the economic sovereignty of their nations; they also tie their own hands politically and deny themselves flexibility in reacting to economic conditions.

Thus a fully neo-liberal world will never emerge, because of the very contradictions and moral bankruptcy of neo-liberalism itself. We can expect increasing struggle taking place between *laissez faire*, social Darwinist conceptions of the appropriate form of state and other models of capitalist social structures of accumulation and industrial organization – for example, the 'Rhineland model' and that of East Asian bureaucratic authoritarian capitalisms, both of which have a more planned, long-term and more productivist orientation than Anglo-American capitalisms (Albert, 1993). It may be no coincidence that the more neo-liberal forces win the struggle over the appropriate political form for capital accumulation, the more social inequality – including gender inequality – tends to deepen and political conflict intensifies. The broader social Darwinism intersects here with questions concerning the political, social and ecological sustainability of the current situation.

In eastern Europe, the reintroduction of neo-liberal marketization is generating a combination of widespread disillusionment and resentment, sentiments which are to a certain extent reflected in the resurgence of populism, racism, fascism and gangsterism. In present-day Russia, for example, the concept of 'marketization' is increasingly associated with desperation, a massive upsurge in crime and violence, as nuclear power stations begin to decay and collapse, and as state arsenals are plundered of weapons by armed gangs. The 'market' is being reintroduced in the context of a general collapse of law and order.

Structural adjustment in Latin America and Africa, and now in the former USSR, is atomizing many state capacities and is generating new social movements and political parties which may in time come to challenge the thrust of neo-liberal orthodoxies. Some of these forces will be ecologists, women's movements and traditional workers' organizations and trades unions. Not all of these movements and parties will represent beneficent trends in world politics: some, such as the far right in Russia, will be malignant elements.

When this is related more broadly to the turmoil in the Third World it gives grounds for considering whether the emerging world order is socially and ethically sustainable. Yet the world is increasingly interdependent both economically and ecologically. Political turbulence and growing disparities in living conditions are driving unstoppable waves of migration. The governments defending the regions of privilege will be hard pressed to cope with or to contain such pressures. To stem such migration requires a more just and egalitarian economic and political structure to the emerging world order.

Thus, whilst there has been some democratization in the 1980s and early 1990s (for example, in some of the bureaucratic-authoritarian nations referred to as the newly industrializing countries [NICs], such as South Korea and to a lesser extent Taiwan), at the same time there has been a worldwide growth in authoritarianism and populism, and a resurgence of fundamentalism (with negative implications for women) of both metaphysical and social types; in this sense, the 1930s and the 1990s are in some ways comparable. Part of the reason for this is that in much of the Third World the processes of urbanization and economic decline have gone with social chaos, anomie and nihilism (Vieille, 1988), although in the NICs they have gone with rapid economic growth and the creation of a civil society which can begin to countervail the unfettered power of the state and the monopolistic producers. China, of course, with its massive and rapid economic growth since the late 1970s is a case of a country in which many of the contradictions associated with commodification and democratization have begun to surface, and where the economic situation seems on the verge of spinning completely out of control.

Elsewhere in the Third World, new types of politics are developing, some relatively invisible and outside traditional conceptions of political action, in a silent revolution of the apparently powerless against those who oppress them. And their oppressors are not just in the G7 countries; they are mainly at home – those urban elites, cadres and ruling classes who are, as I have mentioned, the principal beneficiaries of loans from the World Bank and aid projects from the richer countries.

Whereas the leaders of the G7 countries appear unable to contain the rise of new right-wing forces which challenge the status quo within their own territories and to reverse the widespread disillusionment and alienation with 'normal politics', many in the Third

World – and not just women – are taking responsibility for their own survival and beginning to exercise social choices which reflect their own interests. It is in this sense that Yoshikazu Sakamoto (see his contribution to this collection, Chapter 6) speaks of the 'powerlessness of the powerful' and the 'power of the powerless'. In this process, then, the poor are not powerless: they have the capacity not only to disrupt the privileged islands of production and consumption, but also to practise 'everyday forms of resistance' to totalizing forces and political and social domination (Scott, 1993).[3] Another indicator of the power of the apparently poor and powerless is the new forms of multilateralism which have begun to emerge among the 'poor' and 'marginalized', to challenge the multilateralism of the powerful (for example, the indigenous peoples of Latin America), as well as myriad forms of local cooperatives, associations and programmes. It is important to link both these local and transnational initiatives in a global political process which also involves progressive social movements and parties from the weathier nations.

By contrast, the formal multilateralism of the G7 nexus has gone with a politics of deflation, mass unemployment and social polarization, and in so doing has all but relinquished the legitimacy to govern in the name of world society. In this sense, the old Cold War categories of left and right, and the organized political parties and forms of state which corresponded to this period, appear to look increasingly obsolete as the world enters a new type of world order.

Some of the issues I have raised in this chapter thus relate to the problematic of politics for the 1990s, and the way that we might begin to conceptualize the 'limits of the possible' and consequently forms of transnational political mobilization of a progressive kind. A certain pessimism is necessary to see how the global crisis will develop and open up 'windows of opportunity'. The 'organic intellectuals' of counterhegemonic forces can help, therefore, to prepare the ground for more constructive, rather than destructive, forms of change. Whereas Schumpeter, following Marx, characterized the process of capitalist development as one of 'creative destruction', it is incumbent on the intellectuals not to

dream of impossible utopias but to think creatively and construc-
tively on the basis of an analysis of real historical forces, in order
to begin to contain and transcend the destructive forces and im-
pulses of our age. I do not think I am being too pessimistic when
I conclude that not all the symptoms during the interregnum are
entirely morbid ones.

Notes

I would like to thank David Law for detailed comments, and the partici-
pants in the United Nations symposium in Oslo on 15–16 August 1993 for
their reaction to and reflections on some of the ideas contained in this
chapter. I would also like to thank Professor Björn Hettne for arranging
the opportunity to deliver some of these thoughts to the inaugural meeting
of the Nordic International Studies Association on 17 August 1993.

1. This painting is a mural from the Quinta del Sordo, transferred to
canvas, 1819–23. It hangs in the Museo del Prado. See J.-F. Chalbrun, *Goya*,
Thames & Hudson, London 1965, p. 228.

2. G. Graham, 'World Bank Report Attacks Inefficiency', *Financial Times*,
20 June 1994. The report in question is *World Development Report, 1994: Infrastructure for Development*, Oxford University Press, Oxford 1994.

3. Indeed, Scott cites the example of the Chinese peasantry whose
collective resistance to the power of the state and the mass starvation
associated with Mao's 'Great Leap Forward' effectively forced the post-
Maoist leaders to institute reforms which included the dismantling of the
ruinous collectivization of agriculture. The market reforms which ensued
provided one of the pillars of the 'Four Modernizations' policy of Deng.
This example shows that the problem is not the market *per se*, but the
conditions of its introduction. Today's new China – 'one nation, two systems'
– shows, at least in the coastal regions, the tendency which is built into
market society: to commodify increasingly virtually all aspects of human
life. This appears to be happening in a virtually unregulated and uncontrolled
manner.

References

Albert, M. (1993) *Capitalism vs. Capitalism*, Four Wall Eight Windows, New
York.
Beneria, L., and S. Feldman, eds (1992) *Unequal Burden*, Westview Press,
Boulder, Colo.

Braudel, F. (1981) *The Structures of Everyday Life: The Limits of the Possible*. Vol. I of *Civilisation and Capitalism, 15th–18th Centuries*, trans. S. Reynolds, Harper & Row, New York.

Cox, R.W. (1987) *Production, Power and World Order*, Columbia University Press, New York.

Elson, D. (1992) 'From Survival Strategies to Transformational Strategies: Women's Needs and Structural Adjustment', in L. Beneria and S. Feldman, eds, *Unequal Burden*, Westview Press, Boulder, Colo.

Galbraith, J.K. (1992), *The Culture of Contentment*, Houghton Mifflin, Boston.

Gandy, O.H., Jr. (1993) *The Panoptic Sort: A Political Economy of Personal Information*, Westview Press, Boulder, Colo.

Gill, S. (1990) *American Hegemony and the Trilateral Commission*, Cambridge University Press, Cambridge.

——— (1991) 'Reflections on Global Order and Sociohistorical Time', *Alternatives*, 16, pp. 275–314.

——— (1992a) 'The Emerging World Order and European Change: The Political Economy of European Economic Union', in R. Miliband and L. Panitch, eds, *The New World Order: Socialist Register, 1992*, Merlin Press, London, pp. 157–96.

——— (1992b) 'Economic Globalization and the Internationalization of Authority: Limits and Contradictions', *Geoforum* 23, pp. 269–83.

Gill, S., and D. Law (1989) 'Global Hegemony and the Structural Power of Capital', *International Studies Quarterly* 33, pp. 475–99.

Gramsci, A. (1971) *Selections from the Prison Notebooks of Antonio Gramsci*, trans. Q. Hoare and G. Nowell Smith, International Publishers, New York; Lawrence & Wishart, London.

Gunnell, J.G. (1968) 'Social Science and Political Reality: The Problem of Explanation', *Social Research* 35, pp. 159–201.

MacNeill, J., et al. (1991), *Beyond Interdependence: The Meshing of the World's Economy and the Earth's Ecology*, Oxford University Press, Oxford.

Mather, G. (1993) 'A Blueprint to Reshape Government', *Financial Times*, 5 October.

van der Pijl, K. (1989) 'Ruling Classes, Hegemony and the State System', *International Journal of Political Economy* 19, pp. 3–35.

——— (1993) 'Soviet Socialism and Passive Revolution', in S. Gill, ed., *Gramsci, Historical Materialism and International Relations*, Cambridge University Press, Cambridge, pp. 237–58.

Polanyi, K. (1957) *The Great Transformation* [1944], Beacon Press, Boston.

Scott, J.C. (1993) 'Everyday Forms of Resistance', *PRIME: Occasional Papers Series*, No. 15, International Peace Research Institute Meigaku, Yokohama.

Strange, S. (1986) *Casino Capitalism*, Basil Blackwell, Oxford.

Tickner, J.A. (1991) 'On the Fringes of the World Economy: A Feminist Perspective', in C.N. Murphy and R. Tooze, eds, *The New International Political Economy*, Macmillan, London.

Toffler, A. (1990) *Power Shift: Knowledge, Wealth, and Violence at the Edge of the 21st Century*, Bantam Books, New York.

Vieille, P. (1988) 'The World's Chaos and the New Paradigms of the Social Movement', in Lelio Basso Foundation, eds, *Theory and Practice of Liberation at the End of the Twentieth Century*, Bruylant, Brussels.

5

The Second Glorious Revolution: Globalizing Elites and Historical Change

Kees van der Pijl

1. Introduction

The world situation that has emerged from the fundamental changes in international relations of the recent period – of which the collapse of the USSR was certainly the most dramatic – requires a profound rethinking of the global configuration of forces created by the spread of the capitalist mode of production. Now that its moment of triumph is passing, and war and crisis are causing widespread disillusion with the glib promises of a peaceful and prosperous 'End of History', our historical perspective on the globalization of capital can be considerably sharpened with the benefit of hindsight.

The thesis of this chapter is that the world is in the process of completing a major cycle between the 1688 Glorious Revolution in England and a comparable removal of political impediments to free enterprise, this time on a world scale. This 'Second Glorious Revolution', taking place three hundred years after the original event, displays a series of similarities with the social transformation which, on the threshold of the eighteenth century, prepared England for the Industrial Revolution. However, the consequences of 'liberalization' are vastly different for societies already structured by an effective state authority and public administration, and those in which state and authority are breaking down. In the latter, 'private' forces occupying the social space abandoned by the collapsing state are operating in a violent, shock-like fashion, often displaying a particularly piratical mentality. The sign in the office of a Russian raw-material dealer that reads 'Kill the Poor' (*Newsweek*, 15 February 1993) speaks in this respect for a new generation in the capitalist class.

But while a few are making millions (and are being applauded in the West as the champions of 'economic reform'), the sudden exposure to the vagaries of the 'market' and to processes of rapid mobilization of wealth and labour-power best designated as original accumulation have left the greater mass of the populations involved in a state of shock designated by sociologists as anomie, a loss of all sense of identity and direction, a breakdown of the normative structure (Vieille, 1988). This is not to suggest that the prior situation was by any means idyllic. We are talking about the need to understand the nature of the recent changes of the global political economy, changes which all too easily and in too many cases have been called 'liberation'.

Our contribution is based on the idea that the 1688 Glorious Revolution created a particular *state/society-complex* (Cox, 1986: 205) covering the British Isles, New England and subsequently, the other areas of English settlement – which we will term the *Lockeian heartland*, after the author of the *Two Treatises of Government*. The Glorious Revolution sealed the series of transformations by which feudal forms of social protection had been torn down. As actual production in England was restructured along the lines of private enterprise employing wage labour ('capital'), the commercial and financial links to Europe and America were likewise tendentially restructured into 'circuits of capital' connected to an industrial pivot.

Still in 1860, Britain, with 2 per cent of the world's population, disposed of 40 to 45 per cent of world industrial production. As Senghaas (1982: 29) comments, 'when one considers international society in its entirety, there is no question that since the first industrial revolution in England, the major part of the world … was turned into a periphery and that only a small number of societies have succeeded in withstanding the pressure towards peripheralization and achieved an autonomous, catch-up development.' The typical state/society-complex of the countries successfully resisting peripheralization may be designated, by reference to the authoritar-

ian prelude to Lockeian liberalization, *Hobbesian*, after the author of
the *Leviathan*; thus giving meaning to the notion of 'Glorious Revolution' in the contemporary context.

We will briefly sketch these ideal-types and then analyse the role
of globalizing elites in the evolving relationship between them. We
take it as self-evident that this can only be a summary and preliminary presentation of a thesis to be worked out at greater length
elsewhere.

2. The Hobbesian and Lockeian State/Society-Complexes

(a) Rereading English seventeenth-century political history

Under the Tudors, who laid the foundations for a modern state in
England, local authority resided with justices of the peace recruited
from the aristocracy, their mandate laid down in parliamentary
statutes. This stood in contrast with the situation in France, where
the king ruled by dispatching governors and royal officials to the
provinces (Trevelyan, 1968: 197). This latter system is characterized
by de Tocqueville (1990, I: 86–7) as 'centralized administration', as
distinct from 'centralized government'.

The English combination of centralized government and a general
framework for local self-government left a wide margin for private
initiative, especially once English trade was emancipated from
Venetian and Hanseatic control (Hill, 1975: 74). Accordingly, the
ascendant bourgeoisie (in the English case an aristocracy shifting to
commercial sources of income; and a lesser, commercially oriented
landowner class), developed organically with the spread of domestic
and foreign trade (Lefebvre, 1976: 31). Only when the Stuarts began
to use royal prerogatives such as the granting of trade monopolies
for their personal enrichment – with a disruption of trade as the
consequence – while failing to defend the common interests of the
English commercial classes against their rivals abroad, did a clash
ensue between the rising bourgeoisie and the king.

Cromwell's Roundhead Commonwealth of 1649 established a
state/society-complex in the spirit of Hobbes's *Leviathan* of 1651.

Hobbes (incidentally, a monarchist then in exile) considered the bourgeoisie responsible for the Civil War and favoured a tentacular, self-perpetuating state closely monitoring civil society. This was broadly what was aimed at under Cromwell: local interests were subsumed under the state, executive privilege overwhelmed the rule of law, and measures were taken to synchronize social energies in order to advance English commercial interests, such as the Navigation Act of 1651, which led to war with the Dutch Republic.

In hindsight we may conclude, with C.B. Macpherson (in Hobbes, 1968: 55–6), that 'what Hobbes overlooked and failed to put into his model was the centripetal force of a cohesive bourgeois class within the society. He was so impressed with the divisive and destructive force of the competition for power ... that he failed to see that the model also necessarily generates a class differentiation which can be expected to produce a class cohesion, at least in the class which is on its way up to the top.'

The ascendant bourgeoisie, which supported the measures mentioned (Trevelyan, 1968: 306), after some time indeed began to resent the expansive (and expensive) 'Hobbesian' state and sought to emancipate itself from it. A class oriented (to the degree it became aware of its own function) towards the ideal of a *self-regulating market* could not, of course, allow the state to continue regulating the economy – even if this happened in the name of the market (Polanyi, 1957: 70). Hence a new conflict ensued, this time with the Roundheads, the followers of Cromwell, whom Gramsci (1971: 77) compared with the Jacobins (and, we might add, the Bolsheviks): a vanguard holding the state in trust for the ascendant social class. The Roundheads 'imposed themselves on the bourgeoisie, leading it into a far more advanced position than the originally strongest bourgeois nuclei would have spontaneously wished to take up.'

The Restoration of 1660 displaced them again and restored aristocratic/bourgeois self-government and a market economy regulated by common law – even more emphatically than it restored the monarchy as such (Trevelyan, 1968: 285). The Glorious Revolution of 1688 then sealed this 'Lockeian' state/society-complex against renewed encroachment by the monarchy and the

Church. The resulting state retained a powerful centralized government, for which 'nightwatch' is perhaps an unfortunate term (see
Barratt Brown, 1988: 34ff), but the social basis of which, 'civil
society', henceforth was allowed to determine the course of
development.

(b) Transnational social forces

The determining feature of the Lockeian state/society-complex in
terms of its further growth (interacting with the spread of the
capitalist mode of production) was the actual transnational extension of the bourgeoisie. Three moments may be distinguished in
this movement: (1) the expansion of civil society; (2) the formation
of transnational elite networks; and (3) the effect on interstate
relations.

   The eventual Lockeian state/society-complex rested on a
transnational civil society well before the writing of the *Two Treatises
of Government*. Overseas settlement predated the outbreak of civil
war in England and the establishment of the Hobbesian state.
Religious conflict played its part in emigration, but commercial
considerations were prominent as well. London private houses such
as the Virginia Company and the Massachusetts Bay Company
between 1630 and 1643 transferred tens of thousands of settlers
to North America. With them went the pattern of local self-
government which de Tocqueville equates with democracy (see
1990, I: 31–5). When the activist state set up by Cromwell and the
Roundheads began to interfere directly with colonization as well,
the pattern of state–society relations designated above as 'Lockeian'
was already beyond its power to change (Trevelyan, 1968: 245).

   In the eighteenth and nineteenth centuries, emigration assumed
epic proportions, spreading to Canada, Australia, New Zealand and
Southern Africa. Between 1812 and 1914, more than 20 million
people emigrated from Britain (Gallagher and Robinson, 1967: 237).
Although by then immigrants from non-British descent were nu-
merically stronger in the United States, social and immigration
restrictions served to sustain the dominant position of the 'White
Anglo-Saxon Protestants' (Nederveen Pieterse, 1990: 270). With

the Lockeian pattern transmitted to the new areas of settlement, there emerged a heartland of shared experiences and outlook, irrespective of whether the actual inhabitants of this transnational society were actually conscious of being part of it or not (Trevelyan, 1968: 633). In Britain, public schools were a crucial channel for instilling a sense of this wider context into the younger generation of the ruling class (Mangan, 1986: 52–3 and passim).

The question of consciousness brings us to the second moment, that of transnational elite networks. Of course, actual economic activity created such networks from the time the English ruling aristocracy engaged personally in it. Thus James, the Duke of York and heir to the throne, was governor of the Royal Africa Company and shareholder of the East India Company; he succeeded Prince Rupert as head of the Hudson Bay Company and was himself succeeded by Marlborough (Trevelyan, 1968: 306). Parallel to such joint directorates there evolved transnational networks of power and influence which went beyond the functional connections created by enterprise as such. The oldest of these, apart from religious networks, is Freemasonry. Although clouded in mystery and a favourite target of conspiracy theorists through the ages, Freemasonry actually was a product of the English political history we have been describing. In the late seventeenth century, 'One thing united a majority of politically conscious people ... the need to preserve the gain of the Civil War of 1642–51 – the limitation of the power of the King', Stephen Knight writes in his study on the subject (1985: 21–2). 'The "accepted" Masons [that is, lodge members, not actual craftsmen] of the last quarter of the seventeenth century would appear to have been largely drawn from the type of people most anxious to preserve and to increase the steadily growing influence in society and government of men of quite moderate wealth and standing.' Their role in challenging absolutist tendencies was matched by their anti-papism, which led to Papal condemnations of the lodges.

From the early eighteenth century on, Freemasonry expanded abroad, both to the English-speaking lands and to Europe. The New England colonies and Virginia became pivots in its further spread, and the first Canadian lodge for instance was set up under

Massachusetts jurisdiction (in 1749). British Freemasonry served to bring together the old aristocracy and the bourgeoisie, notably 'the not directly productive and professional middle classes' (Knight, 1985: 37); but the liberal, Lockeian profile travelled with its extension abroad. Thus, while the argument for self-regulating civil society in the *Federalist Papers* reveals its English models in terms of content (W.R. Brock, in Hamilton et al., 1992: xiii), it is also of significance that James Madison was a Freemason (as were George Washington and fifteen other US presidents up to Ronald Reagan [Knight, 1985: 34]). By then, Freemasonry had come to have a wide variety of political contents, as is witnessed by the lodge *Propaganda Due*, which functioned as a right-wing shadow government in Italy and actually took power with the Second Republic inaugurated by P2 member Silvio Berlusconi.

It took until the late nineteenth century before the challenge of strong European contenders, primarily Germany, led to the establishment of more specific and politically focused transnational elite networks in the Lockeian heartland. Their main architect was Cecil Rhodes, the British South African politician and financier, whose life ambition was 'the furtherance of the British Empire, the bringing of the whole uncivilized world under its rule, the recovery of the United States of America, the making of the Anglo-Saxon race into one Empire' (quoted in Shoup and Minter, 1977: 12–13). Rhodes and a circle of like-minded economic statesman with Oxbridge antecedents, such as Lords Esher, Grey, Milner, Rothschild and Balfour, translated their aristocratic, 'ethical racist' concept of an Anglo-Saxon civilizing mission into a secret society of concentric circles of 'Initiates' and 'Helpers'. The latter were reorganized, from 1909 on, into the Round Table groups in the British Empire and the US by Lord Milner. Milner, too, upon Rhodes's death in 1902, organized the Rhodes Trust as a transnational educational network dedicated to Rhodes's ideals (Nederveen Pieterse, 1990: 272–3; cf. Quigley, 1966). The various Rhodes networks have continued to function to the present day, like their offshoots the British Royal Institute of International Affairs and the US Council of Foreign Relations (Shoup and Minter, 1977). Directly and through these institutions, English and US elite universities remained connected into a wider culture of Anglo-Saxon chauvinism. Thus a direct link between the Rhodes Trust and the contemporary political scene can be traced in the careers of both President George Bush and his successor, Bill Clinton, each interfacing with the Harriman banking dynasty in the USA (Reuveni, 1993; on the Rhodes network and the Clinton Administration, see *Newsweek*, 4 May 1992 and 26 October 1992).

The suggestion of a conspiracy theory, which inevitably emanates from such lists of (secret or semi-secret) elite networks and their membership in high places, can be dismissed simply by pointing out that a large part of the world remains beyond the reach of even the most powerful among them. Even the world that they consider their own can only be marginally controlled by them, if 'control' is the appropriate term. Rather, we should view these networks as channels of cultural synchronization and informal policy discussion and preparation. The importance of this becomes clear if we accept the idea that the weight represented by the Lockeian 'West' in world affairs has resided to a considerable degree in its capacity to shape ideological processes of consensus and compromise, related of course to its superior wealth and means of violence. 'Every relationship of "hegemony"', Gramsci writes (1971: 350), 'is necessarily an educational relationship and occurs not only within a nation ... but in the international and world-wide field, between complexes of national and continental civilizations.' Transnational elite networks in this context play a role 'as international political parties which operate within each nation with the full concentration of the international forces'. They should be understood as (collective) 'intellectuals',

> whose function, on an international scale, is that of mediating the extremes, of 'socialising' the technical discoveries which provide the impetus for all activities of leadership, of devising compromises between, and ways out of, extreme solutions. (Gramsci, 1971: 182n; cf. Cox, 1993; Gill, 1991)

This brings us to the effect that the transnational expansion of social forces has (had) on the state system. The centrifugal pattern of state formation that broke up the first and second British

Empires between the American Revolution and the mid-nineteenth-century emancipation of Canada, Australia and New Zealand did not destroy the common civilizational heritage, nor the Lockeian state/society-complex that was part of it. The USA in the nineteenth century passed through a phase of strengthening the state and reinforcing domestic social cohesion, before it made its definitive appearance on the world scene as a great power. This coincided with the quest for Anglo-Saxon unity from Britain; and, as the conflagration with the European challengers began to appear on the horizon, several steps were taken to draw the white English-speaking world closer together politically. In 1911, the Arbitration Treaty between the USA and Britain outlawed war between the two countries. In the same year, Britain, Canada, Australia and New Zealand formed the British Commonwealth of Nations (Hall, 1971).

The formation of this core area and its performance in World War I marked the crystallization of a Lockeian heartland into which other states were to be absorbed and which served as a model for international *integration* both in theory and in practice (cf. overview of theories in this light in van der Pijl, 1995: ch. 9; Monnet, 1976). Integration, first of the Anglo-Saxon world, then spreading to Western Europe after World War II, did not so much create the federalist superstate favoured by some of its supporters; rather, it was meant to further the mutual fine-tuning of national policies and the creation of a common legal framework for the self-regulation of civil society.

In this way, and interacting with the previously discussed trans-nationalization of civil society and of elite networks, integration created a loose and highly flexible structure of sovereign states characterized by the historian of the British Commonwealth as 'a system of interlinked groups, organizations and societies within the greater community [which] was able to avoid in very large measure the growth of rigidities and compartmentalization in its political, economic and social structure' (Hall, 1971: 106).

Victorious in two world wars, and eventually in the Cold War, the Lockeian heartland that grew out of this Commonwealth/US connection led in the late 1980s the final spurt in the century-long process of transnationalization of capital. For a short time, the 'Big Bang' of the 1980s created the semblance of a unified capitalist world.

(c) Contender states and the Hobbesian counterpoint

While in the English-speaking world the rise of a bourgeoisie profited from the strong tradition of local self-government that could survive the Hobbesian transformation, in the countries resisting peripheralization by the Lockeian heartland the strong state, once put into place, proved less easy to transcend. In Britain the bourgeoisie crystallized in revolt against the monarchy, then was drawn into a revolutionary dictatorship by a radical vanguard, only to throw off the encroaching state again when it reached maturity as a class-for-itself in the transnational context. The dialectical moments of this process, what Overbeek (1990) calls the 'long wave of class formation' (national centralization and transnational hegemony), interacted with commercial ascendancy, industrial revolution, and centrality in the global distribution of profit.

In France, the first major contender in the late seventeenth and eighteenth centuries, relative economic backwardness combined with structural disadvantages of a socio-geographic type to congeal the state/society-complex into the 'Hobbesian' configuration the power-holders resorted to in order to catch up with Britain. From the Cardinals and Louis XIV, interrupted by the French Revolution which expressed the accumulated contradictions of the state-driven catch-up attempt, resumed under Napoleon, and henceforth pursuing a pattern of national development reproducing the pre-eminent role of the state in society, interrupted by shock-like adjustments (1848, the Popular Front/Vichy, 1968) and foreign wars, France remained tinged by this formative experience. In contrast to class formation in England, which was set basically in a trans-national, commercial context, in France the state forced the transition towards a commercial-industrial society on the country from above.

'Economics and politics are articulated in the bosom of the state; this state brings forth social relations which react on it, it is the producer and the product of these relations', writes Lefebvre (1976: 36). The 'vanguard' (Roundhead, Jacobin, but also modernizing bureaucracies under royal or military rule) forcing the social formation into its progressive configuration here is not displaced as soon as the ascendant class is 'in place'; it cannot relinquish state power. We will term such a group a *state class* because its power primarily resides in its hold of the state apparatus rather than in a self-reproducing social base (see Cox, 1987: 366–7; Fernández Jilberto, 1988: 55).

De Tocqueville (1990, I: 87) already in the early nineteenth century concluded that such a state in the long run exhausted a country's creative energies, even if it could profit from the total mobilization of resources in the short run. In the case of France, a contemporary critic (Cohen-Tanugi, 1987: 6 and *passim*) has observed that the drain exerted by the tentacular state is today still a brake on society's capacity to engage in transnational competition.

Generalizing from the French example, we may reinterpret the structure of the international political economy between the two Glorious Revolutions as a process of uneven expansion of the Lockeian heartland, challenged by successive generations of Hobbesian contender states. The internationalization of capital, far from taking place (as a 'world economy' concept would suggest) in a fixed landscape of sovereign states representing locations in a global division of labour (for example, Wallerstein, 1979), takes shape in the confrontation, at the political level, with these contenders and in most cases ends with their collapse and subsequent integration into the heartland (see, on Spain, Holman, 1993; on Germany, van der Pijl, 1994; on the USSR, van der Pijl, 1993)

While the heartland has thus expanded by transnational penetration and integration, the Hobbesian contenders have necessarily operated on their own, fighting each other as often as they fought the hegemonic heartland. State-driven (by revolutions from above, generating wars and/or revolutions from below, overtaken again by resumptions of the revolution from above), some of these Hobbesian state/society-complexes have yielded remarkable examples of rapid mobilization of resources narrowing the gap with the more developed West. They have included mercantilist, fascist and

Table 5.1 The Lockeian and Hobbesian State/Society Complexes

	Lockeian	Hobbesian
Privileged terrain of social action	civil society	state
Ruling class	bourgeoisie	state class
Mode of regulation	self-regulating market (civil law)	state-regulated economy (administrative law)
Mode of expansion	transnational	international

state-socialist political regimes, while varieties of nationalism have further complicated the picture. To the extent that they have been capitalist in orientation (in a sense they always were, since their sights were set on catching up with the capitalist heartland), the pre-emptive confiscation of the social sphere by the contender state (although varying greatly between the cases in terms of actual state control) gave the directive state apparatus a place in the social structure precluding liberalism. Therefore, we might employ Henri Lefebvre's (1977) notion *state mode of production* to denote the fact that, although single capitalist firms ('particular capitals') may operate in it, these relate, in the domestic context, not to the self-regulating market ('total capital') as the comprehensive social structure, but to the state. The sovereign state, rather than capital, ultimately determines the status of social actors and constrains, for instance, their capacity to articulate their interests in the transnational space dominated by the Anglo-Saxon ruling class, the flexibility that goes with such informal consultation, and integration. In Table 5.1, the main characteristics of the Lockeian and Hobbesian state/society-complexes are summed up.

Elaborating on André Gunder Frank's 'development of under-development' analysis (Frank, 1975) and Senghaas's theory of 1982, we may accordingly distinguish between a heartland of 'development', the Hobbesian ring of states resisting peripheralization and 'developing' through revolutions from above, and the actual area

Table 5.2   State/Society-Complexes in the 1688–1988 Cycle

Period	Lockeian heartland	Paramount Hobbesian states
1688–1789	England, New England *cum annexis*	France
1789–1870	Britain, self-governing colonies, USA	France, Prussia, Austria-Hungary
1870–1945	USA, British Commonwealth, (France)	Germany, Japan, Italy, Russia/USSR
1945–1988	North Atlantic bloc (West Germany, France), Australia/New Zealand, (Japan)	Soviet bloc, China, India, Mexico, Brazil, Iran...

of 'underdevelopment'. The particular characteristic of the Hobbesian formations would be, then, that the strong states that allow them to hold their own in the confrontation with the heartland cannot be 'organically' transcended because the transnational, 'social' terrain is already occupied by the Western bourgeoisie.

Yet the state classes of various stripe have also to reckon with domestic social forces developing surreptitiously, 'molecularly' in the direction of the pattern prevailing in the heartland; if only as a consequence of the very transformations that are being wrought by the revolutions from above. This process is captured by Gramsci (1971: 114) in his concept of *passive revolution* . At some point (and here the political orientation of the state class and the stringency of state control are, of course, crucial determinants) this social stratum is bound to surface and constitute itself as a class. Capital links, integration into transnational elite networks, and eventually a class struggle with the state class of the type that displaced the Roundheads in seventeenth-century England, will eventually accompany the repeat performance of the Glorious Revolution. This struggle also may involve an opportunistic change of colour, just as part of the Roundhead elite survived as Whig lords under the new order.

In Table 5.2, we have attempted to schematize this complex structure (all along leaving a permeable, exposed periphery). We have followed a simple periodization running from 1688 to the French Revolution, with '1870' a reference to revolutions from above in Japan, Italy and Germany; then the postwar world up to the collapse of the Soviet bloc. Brackets indicate that countries subsequently integrated into the heartland display strong traits from their antecedent Hobbesian experience.

Due to the pre-emptive confiscation of the social sphere by the state, multilateralism among Hobbesian contender states was usually of an additive, often authoritarian, type. These countries, always susceptible to the workings of the 'balance of power' in the sense of being played off against each other by the heartland states, might form blocs like Napoleon's Empire and the Continental System, the Nazi *Reich*, or the Soviet bloc/COMECON, but they retained their Hobbesian antecedents. The final instance of such multilateral/state (instead of transnational/social) collusion was the 1970s drive for a *New International Economic Order* (NIEO), which coincided, mainly on account of rising oil prices, with expanding East–West trade and détente, and with crisis in the heartland.

3. Transnational Elites in the Second Glorious Revolution

(a) Structural trends

The challenge posed by the contender states more or less united behind the concept of a NIEO (of which at least four versions have been distinguished relating to partially different social forces [Cox, 1979]), could be met by the capitalist class from the heartland because a new mode of accumulation began to crystallize in the same period. This new mode of accumulation rested on two pillars. One was the application of *microelectronics* in production, coupled to the resurrection of a 'craft paradigm' on the shop floor displacing standardized mass production (van Tulder and Junne, 1988; Piore and Sabel, 1984). The other was a resurgence of the *rentier*, the 'functionless investor' as Keynes called him; as well as the institutions catering to this social category such as investment

Table 5.3   Most Centrally Located Firms in the International Network of Joint Directorates, 1970, 1976, 1992

Rank	1970	1976	1992
1	JP Morgan (b/US)	Chase Manhattan (b/US)	Citicorp (b/US)
2	Chemical Bank (b/US)	Deutsche Bank (b/G)	GM (i/US)
3	Chase Manhattan (b/US)	Canadian Imp. (b/Can)	AT&T (i/US)
4	Royal D./Shell (i/N-UK)	Chemical Bank (b/US)	IBM (i/US)
5	Deutsche Bank (b/G)	Dresdner Bank (b/G)	CS Holding (b/Swi)
6	Int. Nickel (i/Can)	Ford (i/US)	3M (i/US)
7	AKZO (i/N)	JP Morgan (b/US)	Unilever (i/N-UK)
8	Gen. Electric (i/US)	Swiss Bank Corp (b/Swi)	Hewlett P. (i/US)
9		Volkswagen (i/G)	
10		Royal D./Shell (i/N-GB)	

Note: b = bank; i = industrial firm
Sources: 1970 – Fennema, 1982: 117, Table 5.6; 1976 – ibid.: 191, compiled from Tables 8.8 and 8.9; 1992 – compiled from Mattera, 1992, company data. To render data comparable, 1970 and 1976 rankings (n = 176) are based on the number of firms linked to, and global centrality (mean distance to all firms), in order to discount mere national prominence, possible if n is high. For 1992 (n = 100) the ranking is only by number of firms linked to.

banks, who had been marginalized from the circuit of industrial capital in the 1930s (van der Pijl, 1984: 100–106, 262–5; Fennema and van der Pijl, 1987a).

Confining ourselves to the field of transnational elite networks, the first level at which such networks can be observed is that of the interlocking directorates of internationally operating companies. Firms with a high centrality must be seen not necessarily as the most powerful, but rather as the places which interface with the greatest number of other places in the network and hence are central in terms of strategic information (see Fennema, 1982 for a discussion of problems associated with this type of analysis). The

Table 5.4 Capital Flight from Third World Countries as a Percentage of External Debt, 1976–82, 1985

	1976–82	1985
Latin America		
Argentina	80.5	98
Brazil		14.3
Mexico	54.0	87.6
Venezuela	65.4	100+
Asia		
India	33.3	
Indonesia	34.2	
Malaysia		80
Philippines		44.4
Africa		
Egypt	44.3	
Syria	96.0	
Nigeria		63.1

Sources: 1976–82 – S. Erbe, 'L'evasion des capitaux dans les pays en [voie de] developpement', *Intereconomics*, November/December 1985, as given in Fennema and Van der Pijl 1987b: 73, Table 16; 1985 – calculated from *Business Week* figures in Petras and Brill, 1988: 187, Table 1.

discussion of broader policy issues will have the widest resonance there, so that the question of which kind of firm is at the centre becomes relevant.

In Table 5.3, the centrality structure of the international network is presented for three years (lists are of different length for computing reasons). The trend, first towards a greater centrality of banks in 1976, reflecting, perhaps, their functional preeminence in a phase of restructuring of capital towards a new configuration; and, secondly, the resurgence of American capital in the high-technology field in 1992, corroborates the idea of a restructuring from a Keynesian/'Fordist' mode of accumulation to a micro-electronics/rentier pattern.

Now although some prominent representatives from what we have termed Hobbesian contender states have made their appearance

Table 5.5 Corporations from Newly Industrializing Countries and the USA and Japan on the Top-1000/Top-100 Lists, 1993

Country	Number	Aggregate market value ($USbn)
United States *a*	403	3,204.8
Japan *a*	281	2,533.0
Hong Kong *a*	21	131.5
Mexico	17	73.6
Spain *a*	11	61.4
Taiwan	20	55.5
South Korea	23	48.3
Malaysia *a*	7	38.9
Brazil	12	33.5
Thailand	9	20.0
South Africa *a*	4	19.9
Chile	5	10.8
Argentina	3	9.1
Philippines	4	8.3
Portugal	3	3.9
Turkey	2	2.6
Indonesia	1	1.4

Note: *a* = Countries taken from the 'Global 1000' list; others from Top 100 emerging market companies.

Source: compiled from *Business Week*, 12 July 1993.

on these boards (for example, the Brazilian economic statesman Mario Simonsen, on the board of Citicorp), the way in which elites from this category of states have sought privately to connect into the metropolitan economy is captured better by the figures on capital flight. Banks which lent on a vast scale during the late 1960s and early 1970s often welcomed back part of the same funds as private 'savings'. Table 5.4 gives an impression of the size of this phenomenon. These figures (which should not be read as a trend, due to the use of different sources and the element of estimate present) may be seen as testifying to the loss of interest in maintaining national productive cohesion under state auspices and the shift to private finance, sometimes by the very people who contracted the debt.

A second dimension of the insertion into metropolitan circuits of capital can be seen in the appearance of transnational corporations from former NIEO countries and Asian newly industrializing countries. This would represent an insertion into the circuit of productive capital itself (and not just into the circuit of money capital). In Table 5.5, the emerging corporations from former Hobbesian states are listed with their number and total value, with the USA and Japan listed for comparison. Banks and privatized telecommunications monopolies, *Business Week* comments on the data, are the most numerous industries represented on its 'Emerging 100' list (25 and 7 entries, respectively). On the basis of the data in our Tables 5.4 and 5.5, it can be assumed that a substantial new bourgeoisie has emancipated itself from the previous Hobbesian states (although we have to view this as a protracted process, proceeding unequally in the different regional settings). This bourgeoisie is engaged in privatizing wealth hitherto controlled in some way or other by the state. 'Growth' figures celebrated the world over as a sign of economic health should therefore perhaps be interpreted first of all as a sign of the capacity of this bourgeoisie to appropriate public goods.

An indication of the wealth *expropriated* from society at large in the process of original accumulation in these countries can be gained from their relative decline in GNP per capita in the 1980s. Thus, after the relative advance of the 1970s, GNP per capita in Brazil fell from 17.5 to 12.1 per cent of a weighted average for the heartland (North America, Western Europe, Australia and New Zealand) between 1980 and 1988; in the rest of Latin America, from 21.1 to 9.7; in the Middle East and North Africa from 11.8 to 7.1; in China from 2.5 to 1.8; and in the Soviet Union from 50.5 to an estimated 16 to 24 per cent (Arrighi, 1991: 49, Tables iii and iv; USSR figures from *Statistical Abstract* 1984: 865, Table 1509, and PlanEcon and CIA estimates for 1988/89 provided by H. van Zon). Only countries maintaining state controls, such as South Korea, could sustain their catching-up strategy (12.7 to 20.2 per cent [Arrighi, 1991: 45, Table ii]). But here, too, maverick capitalists are beginning to take a second look at the costly tentacular state (*Business Week*, 1 June 1992).

This breakdown of state control of the economy ('economic reform') is viewed increasingly as the key to 'growth'. 'Increasingly, both the size and the effectiveness of government is being challenged, and nowhere more so than in developing nations', *Business Week* (7 June 1993) writes. 'The fastest growing non-democracies have, in fact, been those countries that have overturned years of government ownership and management of business and extended numerous protections to private property owners – from sensible regulations to lower business taxes.' And *Business Week* explicitly makes a comparison with the political history of the Lockeian heartland, when it continues:

> Such power-sharing and decentralization of government has historically proved a powerful impetus to growth and development: Britain's Industrial Revolution occurred in the 'new' cities of the north, such as Birmingham and Manchester, where laws and regulations in the wake of the Glorious Revolution of 1688 were looser than in the old financial centers, such as London. And in the U.S., rapid growth in the 19th century was propelled in part by a federalist, states' rights system that allowed agriculture and industrialization to thrive free of central control.

The *Financial Times* (29/30 May 1993) even takes the historical reference another century back, when it writes that 'The 1980s look the finest years for would-be *nouveaux riches* since the forebears of many of today's ducal families grew fat on the dissolution of the monasteries.'

Now even apart from the expropriation inherent in original accumulation, the Second Glorious Revolution has been a violent process all along; indeed a class struggle against the forces challenging the hegemony of the West by the NIEO programmes (see Krasner, 1985) as well as by détente between East and West (Gerbier, 1987; Halliday, 1986). On hindsight, the 1973 coup against the *Unidad Popular* government in Chile and the application of monetary and market 'discipline' on society, backed up by state terror, may be seen as the first serious blow dealt to the state-led industrial and redistributive policy (financed by raw-material income and foreign credit) that was the key aspect of most NIEO concepts.

What is more, the new production technologies such as microelectronics were first developed by US defence suppliers (van Tulder and Junne, 1988: 7; Junne, 1985) and then consciously applied in a strategy of achieving a qualitative superiority in the arms race with the USSR. Developing 'a well designed program of economic sanctions' against the USSR was seen explicitly by Assistant Secretary of Defense Richard Perle as a means to 'damage the Soviet economy and slow the growth of their defense industrial base' (quoted in Brownstein and Easton, 1983: 459). Parallel to this, the United States (a *New York Times* report deduced from classified government documents) should develop weapon systems that 'are difficult for the Soviets to counter, impose disproportionate costs, open up new areas of major military competition and [make] previous Soviet investments [obsolete]' (quoted in Gervasi, 1990: 23).

The decision in 1979 to introduce new NATO missiles on European soil, especially the 'Star Wars' project launched in 1983, which served to heighten tension, were key in this strategy, although important owner-managers of US high-tech firms such as Thomas Watson of IBM and David Packard of Hewlett-Packard – corporations moving towards network centrality at the time (see Table 5.3) – had to intervene to ensure that technological advantages were used economically and not just to enrich defense contractors (Junne and van der Pijl, 1986). At the same time as forcing the USSR's back against the wall, the technological revolution in the West and its Asian outposts marginalized Soviet-bloc producers from the heartland economy. COMECON deliveries, which in 1973 still accounted for 22.7 per cent of machinery imports into the OECD area, were by 1985 reduced to 4.9 per cent (Van Zon, 1994: 38).

Meanwhile, decisions such as the 1979 turn to deflation in the USA decreed by the Federal Reserve under the chairmanship of Paul Volcker, followed up in the 1980s by counter-revolutionary guerrilla campaigns under the 'Reagan Doctrine', further added to the crisis of the Hobbesian contenders and those peripheral formations attempting to emulate their example.

(b) Elite planning in transnational networks

Although important differences remain between Hobbesian states trying to work their way into the global circuit of capital centred

Table 5.6 Transnational Elite Networks in the 1688–1988 Cycle

Era and hegemonic concept	Heartland definition	Transnational networks	Paramount Hobbesian states
LIBERAL INTERNATIONALISM			
1688–1789	England, New England c.a.	Freemasonry	France
1789–1870	Britain, self-governing colonies, USA	Rhodes/Milner Group, Round Table	France, Prussia, Austria-Hungary
STATE MONOPOLY TENDENCY			
1870–1945	USA, British Commonwealth (France)	International Chamber of Commerce	Germany, Japan, Italy, Russia/USSR
CORPORATE LIBERALISM			
1945–1973	North Atlantic bloc (France, West Germany)	Bilderberg Conferences, Atlantic Institute, Club of Rome	Soviet bloc China, India,
NEOLIBERALISM			
1973–present	Australia, New Zealand (Japan)	Trilateral Commission, Mont Pèlerin Society, Pinay Circle	Mexico, Brazil, Iran...

Note: Definitions of hegemonic concepts are taken from the introductory chapter in Overbeek, 1993: 7.

on the heartland and states resisting capitalist control and committed to political alternatives (state socialism), the new mode of accumulation and the 'Second Cold War' against obstacles to it across the globe spelled disaster for the contender states. Their crisis was then capitalized on by the advancing forces of the West. As Robinson (1992: 8) writes, 'In every region of the world, states, economies, and political processes are being transformed *under the guidance of a class-conscious transnational bourgeoisie.*'

Now, bourgeois class consciousness has assumed different historic forms, and the original liberalism that inspired the 1688 Glorious Revolution, before it resurfaced as *neo-liberalism* in the 1980s, has undergone several revisions. Elsewhere, we have distinguished two other comprehensive concepts of this kind, each interacting with a particular mode of accumulation and configuration of the bourgeoisie in the heartland (van der Pijl, 1984; Overbeek, 1990, 1993) in addition to this liberalism/neoliberalism: a *state monopoly tendency* expressing the rise of heavy industry and labour corporatism in the early twentieth century, and a postwar *corporate liberalism* based on Keynesian/Fordist mass production and demand management in the context of 'welfare states'.

Such concepts have served to lend cohesion to disparate strategies of economic and political actors, and of course have had very different social and intellectual sources. But transnational elite networks have always been a crucial relay of their articulation, an arena where different strategies have been confronted with each other and a 'collective will' of the forces represented thrashed out, as well as a channel for their subsequent dissemination. Since the Rhodes/Round Table networks, they have become ever more purposeful and sophisticated as they evolved along with the restructuring and expansion of the heartland.

Elaborating on a list given by Gill (1991: 123), Table 5.6 locates elite networks in the chronology of contexts taken from Table 5.2 above. It should be emphasized that all networks mentioned have continued to function ever since the period in which they appeared on the scene (which is given in the table).

Although it would be tempting to elaborate on the ways in which the networks listed (however different in nature, membership and political orientation they may have been) have functioned in shaping the hegemonic forces in the heartland while sustaining the classes progressing 'molecularly' in the passive revolutions in the Hobbesian states, we cannot, for reasons of space, go into this matter here. Otherwise, the role of Freemasonry on the European continent in the eighteenth and nineteenth centuries (Knight, 1985:

26, 32–3), in Latin America in the nineteenth (Nederveen Pieterse, 1990: 135), the role of the International Chamber of Commerce in reintegrating the German bourgeoisie in between the world wars, and so on, would have to be discussed in detail. As to the twentieth-century Atlantic context, the author's 1984 study on the subject could be consulted.

If we confine ourselves to the neo-liberal phase, we may get an indication of the role of transnational elite networks in the process of globalization of capital if we analyse two crucial policy areas referred to in section 3(a) above.

The first is the preparation and propagation of an economic programme meant to displace Keynesian/Fordist corporate liberalism in the West; whether intended or not, this has served to undermine the productive cohesion of the Hobbesian states. In this regard, the Mont Pèlerin Society established in 1947 by Friedrich von Hayek, Milton Friedman, Karl Popper, and others, has developed from a marginal sect of ultra-liberals into a crucial source of neo-liberal propaganda and policy advice. Friedman, president of Mont Pèlerin from 1970 to 1972, advised the Pinochet regime on the application of a monetarist shock-therapy; henceforth, the neo-liberal gospel was spread, directly or through national bodies interlocked with Mont Pèlerin, to countries like Britain (Overbeek, 1990: 28, 162, 164; Desai, 1994) and the United States (through the Heritage Foundation launched in 1973, whose president, Ed Feulner, served as Mont Pèlerin's treasurer since 1978 [*Who's Who in the World, 1982*]). All along, the hegemony of neo-liberal ideology developed along a broad front in the media and academia, receiving its most prestigious seal of approval in Nobel Prizes for Hayek in 1974 and Friedman in 1976. Third World representatives gradually came round to public pronouncements in favour of Pinochet's neo-liberalism in spite of its record for state terror, with Mont Pèlerin serving as a forum (*Hoy*, 25 November 1981). Key figures from the Mont Pèlerin Society still continue to make the headlines when it comes to new instalments of the neo-liberal revolution. Thus, Silvio Berlusconi's Foreign Minister, Antonio Martino, apart from being a member of the P2 masonic lodge, served as Mont Pèlerin's president from 1988 to 1990 (*Volkskrant*, 26 May 1994).

The *Trilateral Commission* (TC), founded in the early 1970s, lacked the doctrinaire unity of purpose of the Mont Pèlerin Society because it was much more a forum dedicated to finding common ground between North American, European and Japanese economic statesmen (Gill, 1991). The idea for a TC including Japanese membership was launched by David Rockefeller, chairman of the Chase Manhattan Bank, the most central firm in the international network of interlocking directorates in that period (see Table 5.3 above) in a Bilderberg meeting. The TC seemed initially committed to a political rather than a market strategy for dealing with the challenges facing the capitalist heartland. Its influential 1975 report, *The Crisis of Democracy*, recommended reducing the 'load' of democratic demands made on the state; in Chile the application of monetarism was argued with reference to this report's claim that authority, especially in economic matters, should be based on expertise rather than democracy (Fernández Jilberto, 1985: 187).

Only later did the TC come round to neo-liberalism, and David Rockefeller in 1979 was instrumental in having President Carter (whose government was so much dominated by TC members that George Bush in his presidential bid of 1980 had publicly to disclaim his membership in order not to spoil his chances with the populist right) appoint former Chase Manhattan banker, undersecretary of the Treasury and TC member Paul Volcker to the chairmanship of the Federal Reserve (Burch 1980, III: 356n). It was Volcker who aligned the USA on the neo-liberal line, effectively terminating the corporate liberal era by the epoch-making deflationary turn in US monetary policy in 1979 (for an analysis of this turnabout critical of the approach used here, see Drainville, 1994: 117 and *passim*).

The second policy area in which transnational elite networks have been active during the neo-liberal offensive, was the actual strategy of confrontation with socialist states, parties, and movements. The two most salient networks active on this dimension were the aforementioned Heritage Foundation and the Committee on the Present Danger (CPD). Both were, strictly speaking, national American bodies; however, they were interlocked densely with transnational networks. The CPD was formed on the waves of a whipped-up panic about Soviet military power in the mid-1970s. It was the single most important network represented in the Reagan Administration, and numbered 32 members, including the President, Secretary Shultz, CIA Director Casey, and others (Brownstein and Easton, 1983: 533–4). Its commitment was to reaffirm the US lead in the arms race by a qualitative shift in weapons technology, backed up by the embargo advocated by Assistant Secretary of Defense and CPD member Perle, which was referred to above.

Heritage was launched with the aid of the populist right (Coors, Mellon Scaife), but also drew support from Chase Manhattan and the big oil companies. It provided Ronald Reagan with a blueprint for his 'revolution', *Mandate for Leadership* (*Guardian*, 25 November 1985). Apart from its links with the Mont Pèlerin Society through Feulner, it was interlocked with the Knights of Malta, a Catholic network dating from the Crusades and including among its members several Reagan cabinet members such as Al Haig and (again) William Casey (see Nederveen Pieterse, 1992). Drugstore tycoon Lewis Lehrman, Heritage Director and Maltese Knight, was the organizer of the tricontinental guerrilla coalition that obtained US government backing in the 'Reagan Doctrine' in 1986 (*Le Monde Diplomatique*, October 1986: 6). The ramifications of this vast undertaking, combining overt and covert operations, involved it with other religious groups and the CIA, as well as arms and narcotics dealers from the Middle East and Central Asia, before it unravelled in the 'Iran–Contra' scandal.

The Pinay Circle, a network with its origins in the European far right and the intelligence services, may be considered the central nexus of European support for a world-wide offensive against socialism (Teacher, 1993). By 1979, it had obtained sufficient respectability to be able to welcome at its Washington conference, among others, Paul Volcker, Ed Feulner, two European Commissioners, as well as key intelligence figures such as former CIA director and organizer of the 'Gladio' undercover network in Europe, William Colby (*Lobster* 17, 1988). Its manifold activities included an abortive strategy to bring Franz-Josef Strauss to power in West Germany, which perhaps illustrates where we should imagine the limits of the power of the networks we have been discussing.

This aspect was brought out also in a Bilderberg meeting in May 1989, when some of the most illustrious North Atlantic economic statesmen discussed the way the Gorbachev phenomenon – and, related to it, the question of Germany – should be dealt with. However, in addition to this and other topics for discussion, a letter from David Williamson, Jr, a senior official from the American space organization NASA, was read out. This outlined a chilling scenario of ecological disaster and planetary crisis for the not-too-distant future, and its final note might well serve as the concluding note of this chapter:

> If there is a challenge to address beyond the technological [the letter concludes] it might be that of finding a philosophy appropriate to a world of universal, interacting scarcities and environmental violence. Man is part of nature; his high[ly] artificial civilization is not. The Bilderberg meeting might wish to spend a moment or two on the response to forces beyond even that assembled power and authority to control. (*Bilderberg*, 1989)

In a world continuing to suffer from the aftershocks of the Second Glorious Revolution – economic ruin, moral degradation and rapidly spreading violence – this might be a sound warning that the social forces from whom a strategy for survival may still be forthcoming should be looked for elsewhere.

Note

The author wishes to thank Ronen Palan and an anonymous reviewer for Zed Books for stimulating comments on the first draft of this paper.

References

Arrighi, G. (1991) 'World Income Inequalities and the Future of Socialism', *New Left Review* 189, September–October.

Barratt Brown, M. (1988) 'Away With All the Great Arches: Anderson's History of British Capitalism', *New Left Review* 167, January–February.

Bilderberg Meetings (1989) La Toja, Spain, 11–14 May (Private collection).

Brownstein, R., and N. Easton (1983) *Reagan's Ruling Class*, Pantheon, New York.

Burch, P.H. (1980) *Elites in American History*, 3 vols., Holmes & Meier, New York and London.

Cohen-Tanugi, L. (1987) *Le droit sans l'Etat. Sur la démocratie en France et en Amérique*, PUF, Paris.

Cox, R.W. (1979) 'Ideologies and the New International Economic Order: Reflections on Some Recent Literature', *International Organization*, vol. 33, no. 2.

———— (1986) 'Social Forces, States and World Orders: Beyond International Relations Theory' [1981], in R.O. Keohane, ed., *Neorealism and Its Critics*, Columbia University Press, New York.

———— (1987) *Production, Power, and World Order. Social Forces in the Making of History*, Columbia University Press, New York.

———— (1993) 'Gramsci, Hegemony and International Relations: An Essay In Method' [1983], in S. Gill, ed., *Gramsci, Historical Materialism and International Relations*, Cambridge University Press, Cambridge.

Desai, R. (1994) 'Second-Hand Dealers in Ideas: Think-Tanks and Thatcherite Hegemony', *New Left Review* 203, January–February.

Drainville, A.C. (1994) 'International Political Economy in the Age of Open Marxism', *Review of International Political Economy*, vol. 1, no. 1.

Fennema, M. (1982) *International Networks of Banks and Industry*, Nijhoff, The Hague.

Fennema, M., and K. van der Pijl (1987a) 'International Bank Capital and the New Liberalism', in M.S. Mizruchi and M. Schwartz, eds, *Intercorporate Relations. The Structural Analysis of Business*, Cambridge University Press, Cambridge.

———— (with J. Ortega) (1987b) *El triunfo del neoliberalismo*, Taller, Santo Domingo.

Fernández Jilberto, A.E. (1985) *Dictadura Militar y Oposición Política en Chile 1973–1981*, Foris, Dordrecht and Cinnaminson, N.J.

———— (1988) 'El debate sociologico-politico sobre casi dos siglos de estado nacional in America Latina: un intento de reinterpretacion', *Afers Internacionals*, 12/13.

Frank, A.G. (1975) *On Capitalist Underdevelopment* [1963], Oxford University Press, Bombay.

Gallagher, J., and R. Robinson (1967) ''The Imperialism of Free Trade' [1953], in E.C. Black, ed., *European Political History, 1850–1870. Aspects of Liberalism*, Harper & Row, New York.

Gerbier, B. (1987) 'La course aux armements: l'impérialisme face au nouvel ordre international', *Cahiers de la Faculté des Sciences Economiques de Grenoble* 6.

Gervasi, S. (1990) 'The Destabilization of the Soviet Union', *Covert Action Information Bulletin* 35.

Gill, S. (1991) *American Hegemony and the Trilateral Commission* [1990],

Cambridge University Press, Cambridge.

——— ed. (1993) *Gramsci, Historical Materialism and International Relations*, Cambridge University Press, Cambridge.

Gramsci, A. (1971) *Selections from the Prison Notebooks*, edited by Q. Hoare and G.N. Smith, International Publishers, New York.

Hall, H.D. (1971) *Commonwealth. A History of the British Commonwealth of Nations*, Van Nostrand Reinhold, London.

Halliday, F. (1986) *The Making of the Second Cold War*, Verso, London.

Hamilton, A., J. Madison and J. Jay (1992) *The Federalist* [1787–88], Dent, London.

Hill, C. (1975) *Reformation to Industrial Revolution*, Pelican Economic History of Britain, Vol. 2, Penguin, Harmondsworth.

Hobbes, T. (1968) *Leviathan* [1651], Penguin, Harmondsworth.

Holman, O. (1993) 'Integrating Southern Europe. EC Expansion and the Transnationalisation of Spain', Ph.D. dissertation, University of Amsterdam (Routledge, forthcoming).

Junne, G. (1985) 'Das amerikanische Rüstungsprogramm: Ein Substitut für Industriepolitik', *Leviathan,* vol. 13, no. 1.

Junne, G., and K. van der Pijl (1986) 'Het tweeledige doel van SDI: militaire superioriteit over de Sovjet-Unie en een technologische voorsprong op de bondgenoten', in P.P. Everts, ed., *De droom der onkwetsbaarheid*, Kok Agora, Kampen.

Knight, S. (1985) *The Brotherhood. The Secret World of the Freemasons*, Grafton, London.

Krasner, S.D. (1985) *Structural Conflict. The Third World Against Global Liberalism*, University of California Press, Berkeley.

Lefebvre, H. (1976) *De l'Etat*, Vol. II, *Théorie marxiste de l'Etat de Hegel à Mao*, 10/18, Paris.

——— (1977) *De l'Etat*, Vol. III, *Le mode de production étatique*, 10/18, Paris.

Mangan, J.A (1986) *The Games Ethic and Imperialism. Aspects of the Diffusion of an Ideal*, Viking Penguin, New York.

Mattera, P. (1992) *World Class Business. A Guide to the 100 Most Powerful Global Corporations*, Henry Holt, New York.

Monnet, J. (1976) *Mémoires*, Fayard, Paris.

Nederveen Pieterse, J. (1990) *Empire and Emancipation*, Pluto, London.

——— ed. (1992) *Christianity and Hegemony. Religion and Politics on the Frontiers of Social Change*, Berg, New York/Oxford.

Overbeek, H. (1990) *Global Capitalism and National Decline. The Thatcher Decade in Perspective*, Unwin Hyman, London.

——— ed. (1993) *Restructuring Hegemony in the Global Political Economy. The Rise of Transnational Liberalism in the 1980s*, Routledge, London and New York.

Petras, J.F., and H. Brill (1988) 'Latin America's Transnational Capitalists and the Debt: A Class-Analysis Perspective', *Development and Change* 19.

van der Pijl, K. (1979) 'Class Formation at the International Level. Reflections on the Political Economy of Atlantic Unity', *Capital and Class* 9.

——— (1984) *The Making of an Atlantic Ruling Class*, Verso, London.

——— (1993) 'Soviet Socialism and Passive Revolution', in S. Gill, ed., *Gramsci, Historical Materialism and International Relations*, Cambridge University Press, Cambridge.

——— (1994) 'The Reich Resurrected? Continuity and Change in German Expansion', in R.P. Palan and B. Gills, eds, *Transcending the State-Global Divide. A Neostructuralist Agenda in International Relations*, Lynne Rienner, Boulder, Colo., and London.

——— (1995) *Vordenker der Weltpolitik*, Leske & Budrich, Leverkusen.

Piore, M., and C.F. Sabel (1984) *The Second Industrial Divide,* Basic Books, New York.

Polanyi, K. (1957) *The Great Transformation. The Political and Economic Origins of Our Time* [1944], Beacon, Boston.

Quigley, C. (1966) *Tragedy and Hope. A History of the World in Our Time*, Macmillan, New York/London.

Reuveni, A. (1993) '"Kein Mensch is in dieser Welt unersetzlich". Hintergründe der politischen Tradition Amerikas', *Das Goetheanum. Wochenschrift für Anthroposophie* 6, June 1993.

Robinson, W.I. (1992) 'The São Paulo Forum: Is There a New Latin American Left?', *Monthly Review* vol. 44, no. 7.

Senghaas, D. (1982) *Von Europa lernen. Entwicklungsgeschichtliche Betrachtungen*, Suhrkamp, Frankfurt.

Shoup, L.H., and W. Minter (1977) *Imperial Brain Trust. The Council on Foreign Relations and United States Foreign Policy*, Monthly Review Press, New York and London.

Statistical Abstract of the United States (1984) Department of Commerce, Bureau of the Census, Washington.

Teacher, D. (1993) 'The Pinay Circle Complex 1969–1989', *Lobster* 26.

de Tocqueville, A. (1990) *Democracy in America* [2 vols, 1835, 1840], Vintage, New York.

Trevelyan, G.M. (1968) *Sociale geschiedenis van Engeland* [1944], Aula, Utrecht and Antwerp.

van Tulder, R., and G. Junne (1988) *European Multinationals in Core Technologies*, Wiley, Chichester.

Vieille, P. (1988) 'The World's Chaos and the New Paradigms of the Social Movement', in Lelio Basso International Foundation, eds, *Theory and Practice of Liberation at the End of the XXth Century*, Bruylant, Brussels.

Wallerstein, I. (1979) *The Capitalist World-Economy*, Cambridge University Press, Cambridge.

Who's Who in the World 1982–1983 (1983), Marquis, Chicago.

Van Zon, H. (1994) 'Crisis in the Socialist International Economy.The Case of Hungary and the GDR', Ph.D dissertation, University of Amsterdam.

6

Democratization, Social Movements and World Order

Yoshikazu Sakamoto

The contemporary world order consists of five key dynamic engines of historical change: one, the internationalization of the state; two, the global penetration of modern science and technology; three, the globalization of the capitalist market economy; four, the universalization of nationalism; and, five, the globalization of democracy and democratization movements. These five are, of course, inter-related, but each assumes the character of an independent variable. What makes the present world order highly problematic is the fact that each of these five dynamics contains a paradox or a contradiction, coupled with the failure to cope with it.

Internationalization of the State

The modern state was built as a new institutional framework to promote the political integration of society when the mobility of goods, capital, persons and information rapidly surpassed the traditional boundaries of fiefs and villages. Now, precisely as the result of the continued promotion of this process undertaken by the state for the very purpose of strengthening the state's power, the mobility of these factors has unmistakably exceeded the boundaries of the state, undermining to a considerable degree the capacity of the state to put these dynamics under its control.

This paradox was tragically demonstrated in 1945 when the nuclear bombs dropped on Hiroshima and Nagasaki foreshadowed the contradiction that the states which possess the weapons of absolute power would absolutely perish. The power of international penetration gave birth to the power of global annihilation. The concept of 'nuclear umbrella' implied the demise of the classical sovereignty of the state defined in military terms. Even the end of the bipolar system did not reverse the trend toward the internationalization of the state. In the multipolar system which ensued, the 'big powers' have not restored the classical system of balance of power but have remained truncated sovereign states. The internationalization of the state in the post-Cold War phase is best illustrated by the mushrooming international institutions and organizations which deal no longer with high alliance politics such as nuclear strategy, but with the issues of 'low politics', of which one of the notable examples is the work of the 'economic summit', that is, G7. In the past, if the presidents and prime ministers of all the big powers assembled, the occasion would be recorded in history textbooks as a historic event which students must subsequently memorize. In fact, a conference involving Great Britain, France, Germany, Italy, the United States, Canada, Japan and the EU (and now Russia) is an event comparable, for instance, to the Versailles Conference in 1919. Yet, today, it is no longer a spectacular event. The way a conference of the heads of the big powers has been routinized as an annual gathering, focused on the issues of low politics, amply demonstrates how deeply the everyday life of the states has been internationalized as business as usual.

One reason for the lack of public attention is the fact that G7, although it is a global economic directorate wielding overwhelmingly dominant economic/financial power over the entire world, has turned out to be ineffective in building a new economic world order. The tendency is a failure to make authoritative decisions, leaving the matter in the hands of bureaucrats. It is so ineffective that, at the G7 conference held in Tokyo in July 1993, the question was even raised by some delegates as to whether G7 should be continued.

The reason is not that G7 has no task to cope with. On the contrary, the task of global coordination of the world economy from the viewpoint of the Northern club of the rich, let alone the poor of the South, is enormous and urgent. The crux of the matter is G7's competence. The causes of its failure are structural. First, the problems – such as nuclear disarmament and proliferation, strengthening of the United Nations, world financial instability, world structural unemployment, global environmental regulations, and so forth – that confront the big powers are of such global consequence that they can no longer be adequately dealt with within the framework of the state system or the mere total sum of the statecraft of individual states. According to some observers and media, G7 is ineffectual because government leadership is weak. But the reality is the reverse: namely, the leadership is weak because the state system is inadequate and incompetent. Further, the triumphant self-congratulatory nature of the victory of liberal capitalist market economy vis-à-vis state socialism is bound to deprive the state of the power and legitimacy of state intervention in the globalized market economy.

Seen from this perspective, it is small wonder that today practically all states – not only weak states in the South and the former East but also the 'advanced' states in the West – are incompetent and ineffectual. This is the powerlessness of the powerful – a contradiction which indicates the erosion of the authority, competence, credibility and legitimacy of the 'sovereign states' in the age of internationalization. Today, while the state and the state system have been considerably incapacitated, international organizations have not acquired the capacity to handle adequately the problems of global importance. To make the situation worse, the states of G7 fall victim to a conceptual inertia and continue to think and act in terms of national interest and state system – a self-defeating response to the global challenge.

Global Penetration of Modern Science and Technology

One of the salient features of developed countries in today's world is the simultaneous presence of destructive power on an unprecedented scale and an unprecedented degree of productivity and consumption. The former is the product of the technology of destruction represented by the nuclear and high-tech weapons systems, which have the potential to annihilate the human species many times over.

The implications of this state of affairs can be appreciated by noting the following point. If any country in the pre-1945 period – the age of conventional weapons – had intended to exterminate the whole human race even only once, that country would have had to devote such an astronomical amount of money and resources to military purposes that the nation would have suffered economic and financial bankruptcy and the people of that country would have had to accept a lowering of the living standard to the level of absolute poverty. For instance, Japan's military expenditure in 1944, when the country was in the last phase of wartime mobilization, was 42 per cent of GNP; yet, while it was totally incapable of conquering even the Asia-Pacific region, the people began to suffer from malnutrition due to food shortage.

In the nuclear age ushered in in 1945, however, the science and technology which gave birth to unprecedented power of destruction also gave rise to unprecedented power of production, particularly in the North. Consequently, the people in the North, while exposed to the danger of species extinction, enjoyed a prosperity unprecedented in history. The result of this affluence was that they were able apparently to forget the danger of massive destruction. This is not simply a matter of forgetfulness or oversight, however; the very structural condition which generated the catastrophic danger made it possible for them to forget about the real danger of catastrophe.

As the danger of nuclear annihilation has receded with the ending of the Cold War, it has become all the more clear to us that it is not only science and technology for military purposes but also science and technology for 'peaceful purposes' which perform destructive functions with regard to the environment. The nuclear catastrophe and the ecological catastrophe have one characteristic in common: both make it difficult for humankind to survive. But there are significant differences.

(1) While catastrophe resulting from nuclear war has been in the realm of possibility, ecological catastrophe is a matter of probabil-

ity. In other words, while the possibility of nuclear war could remain more or less on the same level for a relatively long period of time, the danger of environmental catastrophe is cumulative and is bound to grow every day unless and until effective remedial measures are taken globally.

(2) Whereas the alternative to nuclear war is obvious, namely non-war and, in that respect, the status quo, the same is not true of the latter because economic non-growth or non-development will give rise to a very serious problem. While non-war will contribute to economic development, non-development will run counter to economic development. It is far more difficult to identify an alternative to development than to find an alternative to nuclear war.

(3) While it is difficult to legitimate nuclear war, it is far more difficult to de-legitimate economic development. Today, every member of humankind has become convinced that he/she has 'the right to development' as a cardinal component of human rights.

In short, it is thanks to the development of modern science and technology that economic development has been made possible on an unprecedented scale; but it is precisely as a result of this economic development that the ecological foundation of economic and human development is being undermined. However, thanks to the economic development made possible by modern science and technology, we can, at least for the time being, forget, ignore or evade the environmental implications of the economic development from which we benefit. There are two problems involved. First, there is a gap between the critical realities and our ostrich behaviour; second, the objective scientific and technological conditions which gave rise to this gap tend to make us forget or ignore it. This is the paradox or contradiction peculiar to the global penetration of modern science and technology.

Globalization of the Capitalist Market Economy

As is well known, while the 'advanced countries' in the North have acquired high economic productivity unprecedented in history, the less developed countries in the South are afflicted by massive poverty, with 400–500 million people – approximately one-tenth of the world's total population – suffering from hunger and fatal malnutrition. The present world order is characterized by the simultaneous presence of unprecedented levels of affluence and of poverty and hunger.

If humankind lived in one country, with the richest top 10 per cent of the total population residing in the Northern suburbs called OECD, while the bottom 10 per cent lived in the Southern shanty towns on the brink of death from hunger, and the next 30–40 per cent up poverty-stricken, this reality would be considered a *political* problem, drawing the attention of the public to the question of political accountability. It might even give rise to a revolutionary situation. But when this bottom 10 per cent is located in developing countries which appear 'remote', people in the North tend to pay little attention to the daily genocide of deprived people and infant children in the South. It is true that people in the North are not totally unconcerned about the poverty and hunger in the South. But their interest tends to take the form of 'charity' and one-off programmes, such as a charity rock concert, sporadic donations, and so forth. Their interest seldom translates into political action that raises the issue of political accountability involved in the global structure of North–South inequity. The persistent lack of interest on the part of people in the North, however, does not necessarily imply that they are terribly selfish and inhumane, with little sense of compassion. The question does not necessarily involve a subjective dimension. The primary reason for the general lack of interest is structural and objective.

According to the logic of capitalist development that has brought about the affluence of the North, there is no economic necessity to save and help the starving 10 per cent of the world's population. For the world capitalist system, these people are structurally dispensable or disposable. If they die from hunger, there will be no adverse effect on world capitalism. Indeed, world capitalism might even be better off if it could save the expenditure on development aid for those people it does not need as part of its drive for economic growth and efficiency.

In sum, then, the fundamental paradox here is that the very

structure which has given rise to the global disparity makes it possible for the people in the North to forget, ignore or evade the problem.

Universalization of Nationalism

In the context of the decolonization that has been under way in the post-World War II period, the collapse of the Soviet empire marked the final phase of the long process of the universalization of nationalism, leading to the eruption of ethno-nationalist conflict. There seems to be a paradox, however, in the process of universalization of nationalism that is under way, in the sense that it indicates the beginning of the end of traditional nationalism. 'Traditional nationalism' refers to the political policy and movement aimed at establishing a sovereign state, the boundary of which is identical to that of the cultural national community.

Precisely as a result of the universalization of nationalism, it has become unmistakably clear that the building of a nation-state on the classical model of self-determination of every ethno-national group is impossible. If such is implemented by force of arms, it will lead to violence and bloodshed, which is self-defeating for the interests of the very ethno-national groups themselves. The horrible devastation and ethnocide in former Yugoslavia is a case in point. The policy of ethnocentrism, as illustrated by ethnic 'cleansing', is self-destructive, particularly in an era of rapidly increasing universalization of international migration and relocation of refugees. Multiethnic, multicultural society is not only necessary but inevitable.

It may be noted in this connection that there seems to be a myth gaining currency in today's world: that the East–West ideological conflict has been replaced by much deeper existential ethno-cultural or civilizational conflict, between Christian, Eastern Orthodox, Islamic, Hindu, Confucian, and other civilizations, and that groups of different ethno-cultures are bound to generate conflict, to fight and eventually to kill each other. This is a civilizational determinism which is false on two counts.

(1) Although there are significant differences in the cultures of

different ethno-cultural groups, cultural difference is not the same as cultural conflict. The question to be addressed in a suitably scientific way should be: Under what conditions will groups of different cultures come into *conflict*? And under what conditions will the conflict turn into *violent* conflict? Since there are a number of instances where people of different cultures coexist peacefully, the shift from difference to conflict and from conflict to armed conflict cannot be accounted for in terms of cultural difference itself, considered as a constant.

(2) The very notion that civilizational difference is existentially irreconcilable and therefore generates deadly conflict is in itself a reflection of a particular kind of civilization, namely, one character-ized by monotheist universalism. It is small wonder that civilizational determinists tend to be obsessed with the conflict between Christianity and Islam. Civilizations characterized by polytheism, which lacks the spirit of crusading universalism, such as Buddhism, Hinduism and Confucianism, can, all else being equal, be eclectic and pluralistic in regard to other civilizations. The universalist notion of the inevitability of civilizational conflict is likely to perform the function of a self-fulfilling prophecy.

Ethno-cultural difference will turn into acute conflict and people will begin to resort to violence when the disparity between the privileged and underprivileged, the rich and poor, the employed and unemployed coincides with, and is based on, a distinction in terms of ethno-cultural and national background, defining the situ-ation in terms of a perceived zero-sum game. This is demonstrated by the fact that most of the ethno-national armed conflicts today are taking place in the less developed regions, including part of the former Eastern bloc, characterized by poverty, inequity and the scramble for scarce resources. What is critical is essentially the lack of equality and equity.

Despite the presence of structural cleavages within ethno-national groups, the question arises: why do people tend to perceive them-selves as constituting a unified group in the face of the perceived hostility of the other ethno-national group? A close examination of the escalation process of ethno-national conflict will reveal that in most cases it is led by a group of extremists, generally small in number at the beginning, seeking to pursue particular interests, who manipulate and inflame the ethno-nationalist feelings, fear, pride or aggressive emotion of the majority of the population, as against a minority of people who take a position in favour of moderation and inter-group cooperation. There is always an element of 'imagined community' utilized by the extremists for their purposes.

Ernst Renan once said that a nation must have a sense of common suffering in addition to the conflicts and divisions also to be found within that nation. In other words, the internal structure of the groups is such that there are without exception fictitious elements in the perceived internal unity of the ethno-cultural groups in conflict. The aroused sense of collective identity tends to conceal inequality, inequity, and even oppression within the group. There is an unmistakable lack of democratic control and accountability.

If democratic equality and equity are ensured within each group, *violent* conflict between ethno-national groups will be minimized. Cultural difference and diversity will be maintained in a democratized world. A world with one single culture would be dreadful, just as a society of people with the same personality type would be a dystopia. Ethno-cultural difference may give rise to a certain degree of tension, just as the existence of different types of personality generates tension. But tension short of conflict, particularly violent conflict, can be a source of creative democratic dialogue, among groups as well as individuals. We must turn, then, to the question of democracy.

Globalization of Democracy and Democratization

One of the most important historic achievements of the post-World War II world is the establishment of democracy and popular sovereignty as a political norm of universal validity. It has become quite difficult for a political regime to be overtly, if not covertly, opposed to democracy. It is interesting to note that, even during the Cold War period, despite the sharp ideological conflict between the East and the West, both subscribed to the principle of democracy as a source of political legitimacy, albeit interpreted in different ways. The dramatic changes that erupted in the East in 1989 were largely a consequence of disintegration *from within*, which was generated by a critical popular awareness of the intolerable contradiction between the avowed principle of socialist democracy and the non- or anti-democratic practices under state socialism. However, precisely at the moment when the principles of democracy and popular sovereignty gained universal validity, a sense of increasing alienation began to erode the confidence in democracy. This alienation manifests itself in the sense of powerlessness shared by a large segment of the population, not only in societies which are undemocratic but also in 'democracies' themselves.

One of the paradoxes of democratic politics is that the larger the number of actors who come to participate in the policy-making process, the more powerless an *individual* citizen tends to find him- or herself. Whereas the 'people' as a collectivity have in principle become sovereign and powerful, an individual citizen plays only a tiny part in the multitude of actors. That is, a growing discrepancy between rights and power has emerged.

The powerlessness of an individual is, in a sense, the price to be paid for democracy; because, under these circumstances, a single individual can hardly become a dictator. But it also carries the danger of eroding the democracy itself. Further, the sense of political powerlessness is even more deeply felt at the international level. This is a consequence of the growing discrepancy between the problems that are global in nature and the political framework of democracy for dealing with these problems, which remains essentially national. This is a gap between the global problematic and national democracy.

What is more, the problem is further complicated by the disparate nature of the issues. In the case of nuclear armament and disarmament, for instance, the focus of the anti-nuclear citizens' movement could be clearly defined because the source of danger was primarily located in the two superpowers – the White House and the Kremlin. When it comes to the issue of the North–South gap and global ecological decay, however, the focus of citizens' actions and popular movements is bound to be diffuse as the locus of political accountability tends to remain ill-defined. In other words, in the case of nuclear armament the problem lies in the presence of the centralized bipolar global power structure; but the North–South disparity and environmental degradation are characterized by the absence of a centralized global power structure that can easily be identified as accountable. In the absence of a clear focus of democratic control by the people, doubt about the efficacy of democratic movements is likely to grow. Herein lies the paradox of the globalization of democratization.

A Silent Revolution from Below?

In sum, internationalization of the state, the global penetration of modern science and technology, the globalization of the capitalist market economy, the universalization of nationalism, and the globalization of democracy are all dynamics that are the product of modernity and have resulted in the paradox that their full-fledged development has brought about self-defeating contradictions. What is the way out?

In modern times, the primary actor constituting world order was the sovereign state. Now that state sovereignty has been eroded and has become diffuse in the context of internationalization and subnationalization, the primary point of reference is being shifted to the people. This is illustrated by the fact that, in the long-standing fundamental tension in modern history between state sovereignty and human rights, the balance is being tipped in favour of the latter. The establishment of international institutions such as the European Human Rights Commission and Court, and the recent debate in the UN on humanitarian intervention, are cases in point. They reflect the deep undercurrent of the globalization of democracy. But, as mentioned above, the globalization of democracy tends to foster a sense of powerlessness on the part of individual citizens.

It was precisely in order to overcome this contradiction of global democracy that new critical social movements emerged in the West, the East and the South. Let me make the following four points in this connection.

First, the democratization movement is not isolated from other social movements. In fact, democratization has never been promoted and achieved by the democratization movement alone. The peace movement, the feminist movement, the environmental movement, the movement against poverty and hunger, the human-rights movement – all are part and parcel of the democratization process. The immediate issues taken up by a specific movement may vary. It is only under special circumstances that these movements converge into a movement specifically focused on political democratization, as dramatically demonstrated in Eastern Europe in 1990. But these critical movements always contribute to democratization, not only of the state but also of the much deeper social base of the state, such as the corporation, workplace, school, hospital, family, and so on.

Second, social movements, particularly the so-called 'new social movements' in the West (and, to a lesser extent, in Japan), are based, in the final analysis, on the demand for the realization of the rights of the individual. This is the essence of modernity, and there is much to appreciate and treasure in this legacy. (I, as a person who was brought up in a semi-feudal, ultra-nationalist, militaristic society and culture, do not have the slightest inclination to underrate the value of modern individualism.)

Yet, the assertion of the *rights* of the individual can, in a subtle way, be equated with the assertion of the *interests* of the individual. This is particularly true when the rights of the individual are vindicated under the capitalist market economy where the assertion of rights tends to be transformed into the assertion of competitive interests. If *rights* which should be universal and public are transfigured into *interests* which are particularistic and private, the movement falls victim to the pitfalls of divide-and-rule and the people are subject to fragmentation. Just as the state has become diffuse, the movement will also become diffuse. The general decline of the interest-oriented labour movement in the West and Japan is a case in point. The interest-oriented movement contains within itself the seeds of its own fragmentation.

The modernist assertion of personal 'ego' is illustrated by the strong emphasis put on the concept of 'self': 'self-help', 'self-government', 'self-determination', 'self-management', 'self-reliance'. Of course, there is nothing wrong if 'self' refers to autonomy and spontaneity. But the question arises: whose autonomy, whose spontaneity? Should it be only that of the individual? I say this not only because I believe this to be one of the sources of weakness of new social movements in the West, but also because I suspect that the contradictions of modernity referred to above cannot be overcome unless modernist individualism is radically re-examined in order to create human and social *solidarity* on a transnational scale.

Third, while critical social movements in the West are relatively weak and inactive today, particularly due to economic recession, there are an enormous number of very active grassroots movements in the South, giving rise to slow but steady change at the bottom of the society. Although most of them are small-scale and generally ignored by the Western media, they are the manifestations of the voice of the voiceless poor, women, children and minorities. These movements are not initiated by activists from the North; they are the product of indigenous ingenuity. Let me give you one example: the Grameen Bank in Bangladesh.

Given that no banks will lend money to the poorest and none will lend money to poor women, thus putting the poorest women in a position of twofold deprivation, the main target of this programme is the poorest peasant women of Bangladeshi villages. A unit of five families, normally represented by women, get together, bringing whatever small amount of money they have. Listening to the living conditions, needs and plans of each family, they discuss among themselves who should borrow first. Suppose a woman borrows money with which she buys three chickens, which she could not buy with her own savings, and farms them so that she can sell them and also produce eggs to improve the nutrition of her children. By selling the chickens she can repay the money she borrowed, even though the interest rate is not low. Then the next woman can borrow money, of which the total amount is larger than the original, and can buy goats which will feed her children with milk; and so on.

Money is lent on condition that no dowry will be accepted or demanded, that children will be sent to the village school, and that no female members of the family will be discriminated against. This is, therefore, not merely an income-generating programme but also a means for spontaneous change of lifestyle through the elimination of inhumane customs and practices. Above all, this is an extremely effective programme for the empowerment of women, who gain confidence in their capacity to lead life with a sense of dignity never experienced before. This is a program of *self*-financing and *self*-employment – but it is a collective self based on mutual support.

The Grameen Bank now has more than one million clients on its books, of which 90 per cent are women. These women have begun to elect their representatives to local assemblies, which will probably extend to the national assembly in the future. This programme, therefore, exists not only for economic development, but also to extend human rights and dignity, and now the practice of democracy. All three are integrated. The significance of this movement to empower women can be appreciated if it is recalled that Bangladesh is a Muslim country.

The initiators of this programme are confident that poverty can be eliminated within a few decades. I have known a number of activists engaged in the struggle against poverty; but I have not met elsewhere people who are so deeply convinced, on the basis of their achievements, that the world's poverty can be eradicated from the grassroots level without much assistance from outside. In fact, this Grameen Bank model has been increasingly replicated with necessary modifications in the Philippines, Indonesia, Malaysia, and other Asian countries, and also in parts of Africa. In essence, this peasant bank represents a silent revolution from below.

This leads to the fourth and final point. Even though we cannot see the visible signs of a great revolution which might change the present world order to one that is more humane, equitable and sustainable, we can hear countless underground rumbles all over the world which presage a global transformation.

It would seem that the days are gone when great leaders put forward the grand design of a new world order and the revolutionary transitional strategy to get from here to there. Instead, it appears that once certain conditions are right and developments converge, people's movements will generate enormous synergic dynamics to achieve a change of a kind that no one has forecast. This is the mode of change of the world order which will take place as part of the process of global *democratization*.

In this context, we can now say that the sense of powerlessness of the individual citizen, on the one hand, and the revolutionary transformation premeditated by no one, on the other, are two sides of the same coin. In place of the theory of change based on a calculated mobilization, which is simply the reverse of modernist technocratic management and engineering, we must reconceptualize global change in terms of a model analogous to the chaos model in mathematics.

It is from this perspective that, despite the diffuseness of the role played by the state, market and international organizations, we can entertain a vision of a democratic world order which is not a fixed institution but a historical process through which the contradictions of modernity will be dialectically overcome by popular forces of global democratization.

About the Contributors

Robert W. Cox, Professor of Political Science and Social and Political Thought, York University, Toronto, has written widely on and changed the frontiers of international political economy, international organization, labour, and theory of political and social analysis. He is the author of *Production, Power and World Order: Social Forces and the Making of History* (New York: Colombia University Press, 1987). A collection of his essays, *Approaches to World Order*, will appear shortly (Cambridge: Cambridge University Press, 1995).

Stephen Gill, Professor, Department of Political Science, York University, Toronto, has written a large number of articles and books on international political economy/international relations. He is the co-author of *Global Political Economy* (Baltimore: Johns Hopkins University Press, 1988), author of *American Hegemony and the Trilateral Commission* (Cambridge: Cambridge University Press, 1988), and the editor of *Gramsci, Historical Materialism and International Relations* (Cambridge: Cambridge University Press, 1993).

Björn Hettne, Professor, Department of Peace and Development Research at the University of Göteborg (PADRIGU), Sweden, has written on colonial history in India, European integration, ethnic conflicts, international relations and development theory. His previous publications with Zed Books are *Development Theory in Transition* (co-author, 1984) and *Europe: Dimensions of Peace* (editor, 1988). His most recent publication is *Development Theory and the Three Worlds* (London: Longman, 1995).

Kees van der Pijl, Reader, Department of International Relations and International Law, University of Amsterdam, has published on European integration, transatlantic relations and North–South issues. Among his publications are *The Making of an Atlantic Ruling Class* (London: Verso, 1984) and, as editor, 'Transnational Relations and Class Strategy' (special issue of *International Journal of Political Economy*, Fall 1989).

James N. Rosenau, Professor, Department of International Relations, George Washington University, Washington DC, is one of the world's most noted scholars of international relations. Among his many publications are *Turbulence in World Politics: A Theory of Change and Continuity* (Princeton: Princeton University Press, 1990).

Yoshikazu Sakamoto is Professor Emeritus, University of Tokyo, and Senior Research Fellow, Peace Research Institute, International Christian University, Tokyo. A distinguished Japanese peace researcher, he has written *Strategic Doctrines and Their Alternatives* (New York: Gordon & Breach), and edited *Asia: Militarization and Regional Conflict* for the United Nations University (London: Zed Books, 1988) and most recently *Global Transformation: Challenges to the State System* (Tokyo: United Nations University Press).

Index

agribusiness interests, 71, 91
Albert, Michel, 71
American way of life, 43
anarchy, 1, 12
anomie, 101
Arbitration Treaty (1911), 108
'asabiya, 45
Australia, 104, 108

Baker, James, 73
Balkan crisis, 16
Bangladesh, 73, 141–2
banks, 114, 116, 117; central,
    independence of, 79; centrality
    of, 115; peasant, 142
Bentham, Jeremy, 88
Berlusconi, Silvio, 106, 122
Bilderberg meetings, 123, 125
biosphere, 41–3; aggressive human
    actions against, 42
black economy, 84
blocs, 4, 113
bourgeoisie, 106, 117, 121; rise of,
    102, 103, 109
Braudel, Fernand, 3, 35, 68, 87
Brazil, 117
Bretton Woods system, 15, 19, 20
British Commonwealth, 108
Buchanan, James, 83
Bull, Hedley, 36, 37
Bush, George, 42, 107, 123

Canada, 72, 104, 108, 130
capital: circuits of, 101;
commodification of, 4; flight
from Third World, 115; growing
power of, 69, 70, 75, 85;
restructuring of, 74, 115;
transnationalization of, 109, 110
capitalism, 5, 9; brutalizing phase of,
    71; competing, 71; reshaping of,
    37; social-democratic, 38
Carter, Jimmy, 123
Casey, William, 124
centralization, 55; of databases, 84
centre–periphery relation, 9, 101,
    111
change: global dimension of, 84;
    historical, 129; holistic
    understanding of, 14;
    structural, 13 (problem of,
    34–5); study of, 1
chaos, 1, 22, 46, 95; organized, 23,
    69, 70
Chase Manhattan Bank, 123, 124
Cheru, Fantu, 41
children, 91, 92; malnutrition among,
    92
Chile, 72, 118, 122
China, 42, 95, 117
citizenship: altruistic, 58; apathetic,
    58; democratic, 58, 62; forms of,
    55–62; ideological, 58; self-
    centred, 57
civil society, 4, 85, 95; expansion of,
    104; global, 86
Civil War, English, 103, 105
class, state-, 110, 112

class formation, long wave of, 109
class struggle, 39
Clinton, Bill, 90, 107
Colby, William, 124
Cold War, 16, 19, 20, 37, 53, 65, 108, 132, 137; Second, 120
collective action, 60, 67, 68
COMECON, 113, 119
Committee of the Present Danger (CPD), 123, 124
commodification of social relations, 87–93; gender bias of, 91
communications networks, global, 37
communism, collapse of, 66, 70
competitiveness, 39, 79
constitutionalism, new, 78, 79, 83, 93
consumption models, 43, 87, 131
Council of Foreign Relations (US), 106
Cox, Robert, 3, 6, 12, 14, 22, 24, 68
credit, for poor women, 141
crime, increase in, 83, 94
critical school, 9, 10
culture of contentment, 36, 73, 89

de-commodification, 88
debt: crisis, 80; Third World, 84
decentralization, 54, 55
decolonization, 135
Delors, Jacques, 16, 82
democracy, 36, 61, 104; deficit of, 16; globalization of, 137–9; liberal, 77; paradoxes of, 138; socialist, 138
democratization, 95, 129–43; globalization of, 23, 24
dependency theory, 9
depoliticization, 36
deregulation, 39, 81, 93
desertification, 41
development, crisis of, 70
dialectic, 35, 56; as causal force, 53; democratic, 61
directorates, interlocking, 114, 123
disorder, 1, 12

dissolution of the monasteries, 118
double movement, 5, 11, 20, 22, 23, 39, 65–99

Earth Summit (1992), 42
earth, photograph of, 47, 49
East Asian model, 94
East India Company, 105
Eastern Europe, 94, 140
economic aspect, 2, 5, 8
economic boom and bust, 59
economic development, dynamics of, 7
economic value, source of, 7
educational opportunity, 59
elite planning, 119–25
elites, 95; global, 100–28; transnational, 105, 107, 113–25
Elson, Diane, 92
English language, 46
environmental destruction, 41, 42, 61, 92, 125, 131, 132, 133, 138
environmental neo-colonialism, 42
ethnic cleansing, 135
ethnic minorities, 55
ethno-national conflict, 136, 137
Europe, 38, 80, 108; NATO missiles in, 119; new, 16; undermining of union, 79; Western, 18
European Bank for Reconstruction and Development (EBRD), 84
European Community (EC), 50, 130
European Human Rights Commission, 139
Exchange Rate Mechanism (ERM), 80
export-processing zones, 91

fascism, 21, 65, 67, 70
Feulner, Ed, 122, 124
finance sector, 69, 81, 85; disciplining power of, 81; interests of, 77; restructuring of, 75–8
fish stocks, decline of, 42
flexible working practices, 90
foetus, photograph of, 47, 49

Fordism, 76, 88, 115, 121; displaced, 122
fragmegration, 22, 54, 56, 60, 61, 62
France, 79, 102, 109, 110, 130
Freemasonry, 105, 106, 121
French Revolution, 109, 113
Friedman, Milton, 122
Friggerio, Paul, 54
Fukuyama, Francis, 36
functionalism, 34
fundamentalism, growth of, 95

Galbraith, J.K., 36, 73, 89
GATT negotiations, 71
Germany, 7, 54, 82, 106, 113, 122, 124, 125, 130
Gill, Stephen, 23, 24, 121
Gilpin, R., 14
Gladio organization, 124
global apartheid, 41
global warming, 42
globalization, 17, 19, 24, 36, 39, 40, 44, 85; as driving force of history, 53; dynamics of, 44–64; economic, 77; of capitalism, 78, 100; of elites, 100–28; of Lockeian state/society configuration, 23; of market, 129
Glorious Revolution: of 1688, 100; second, 100–28
government, redefinition of role of, 86
Grameen Bank, 141–2
Gramsci, Antonio, 3, 4, 9, 23, 24, 35, 65, 66, 85, 103, 112
Gramscianism, 14, 22, 86
Great Transformation, 11, 14, 19, 66–7
The Great Transformation, 4
Group of 7 (G7), 81, 95, 96, 130; competence of, 131; nexus, 86
Gulf War, 72–3
Gunder Frank, André, 111

Haig, Al, 124
Harriman family, 107
von Hayek, Friedrich, 122
health care, privatization of, 90

Hegel, G.W.F., 44
hegemonic stability, 14, 16, 17
hegemony, 4, 18, 65, 107; counter-, 93–7; importance of, 14–15
Heritage Foundation, 123
historical materialism, 67
historical structures, 33, 68
history, end of, 36, 100
Hobbes, Thomas, 23, 86, 102–13
Hudson Bay Company, 105
human rights movement, 140
hyper-consumerism, 88
hyper-liberalism, 37, 38

Ibn Khaldun, 45
identities: ethnic, 39; gender, 39
individual, 141; rights of, 140
individualism, value of, 140
Indonesia, 142
Industrial Revolution, 100, 118
information technology, 59
insecurity, 87–93
institutionalism, neo-liberal, 17
interdependence, 19, 46; global, 17
interest, rising rates of, 80
International Chamber of Commerce, 122
International Monetary Fund (IMF), 37, 71, 73, 84
International Political Economy (IPE), 1, 8, 17–21, 32; and transformation, 10–17; liberal, 8–9; Marxist, 9; new, 5; realist, 9–10
interregnum, theorizing of, 65–99
intersubjective meanings, 33–4
intersubjectivity, 35, 67; shift in, 39; void in, 36
intervention, 19, 37; restriction of, 39
invisible hand, 44
Iran–Iraq war, 72
Islam, 43, 136, 142
Italy, 54, 55, 106, 113, 130

Jacobins, 110
James, Duke of York, 105

Japan, 16–17, 18, 38, 72, 75, 78, 82, 113, 116, 117, 130, 132, 140

Keohane, R.O., 14, 17
Keynes, J.M., 76, 113
Keynesianism, 76, 77, 88, 115, 121; displaced, 122
Kindleberger, C., 14
Knight, Stephen, 105
Knights of Malta, 124

labour movement, 140; weakening of, 40
labour: commodification of, 4; decline of organized power, 76
laissez faire, 73, 81; spread of, 69
Lefebvre, Henri, 111
legitimacy, decay of, 36
Lehrman, Lewis, 124
Leviathan, 102
liberalism, 7, 14, 131; corporate, 121 *see also* hyper-liberalism *and* neo-liberalism
List, F., 7
literacy, 74
localism, 20
localization, 47; dialectics of, 49–55
Locke, John, 23, 86, 102–13
longue durée, 87
lumpenproletariat, growth of, 91

Maastricht Treaty, 16, 72, 79
Machiavelli, Niccolò, 10, 45
Macpherson, C.B., 103
Madison, James, 106
Malaysia, 142
malnutrition, 92, 134
Maquiladoras, 78, 91
marginalization, social, 5, 40, 70, 75, 77, 78, 88
market, 101; common, 18; concept of, 4; destabilizing effect of, 11; discipline of, 85, 93, 118; expansion of, 11, 50; globalization of, 133–5; intensification of, 78; logic of, 2; penetrative power of, 5;

presupposing order, 15; self-regulating, 39, 81, 86, 103; system, 4
market exchange: moral neutrality of, 11; nature of, 12
marketization, in Eastern Europe, 94
markets: finance, 69; mega-, 18
Martino, Antonio, 122
Marx, Karl, 8, 34, 96
Marxism, 7, 10
Massachusetts Bay Company, 104
mediaevalism, new, 36
mercantilism, 6, 7, 82
Mexico, 72, 73, 78, 91
micro-electronics, 115, 118
migration, 50, 51, 54, 95, 104; mass, 41; urban, 77
Mill, John Stuart, 7
Milner, Lord, 106
modernization, 110; imperative, 7
money, as principal means of social exchange, 87
Mont Pèlerin Society, 122, 123, 124
moral philosophy, 44–5
multilateralism, 17; among the marginalized, 96; new, 21, 23
Multilateralism and the United Nations System (MUNS), 21, 22

nation-state, 21; decline of, 12; self-interest of, 17
nationalism, 129; economic, 18; traditional, 135; universalization of, 135–7
Navigation Act (1651), 103
neo-liberalism, 5, 39, 66, 70, 71, 73, 74, 81, 82, 121, 122; contradictions of, 93–7; countervailing of, 69, 74
neo-Marxism, 14
neo-mercantilism, 19
neo-realism, 14
New International Economic Order (NIEO), 72, 113, 117, 118
New Zealand, 82, 90, 104, 108
newly industrializing countries (NICs), 95, 117
non-development, 133

non-elites, 24
North American Free Trade
    Agreement, 54, 72, 91
Northern League, 54
nuclear umbrella, concept of, 130
nuclear war, catastrophe of, 132
nuclear weapons, 129, 132, 138

oil producers, power undermined, 72
ontology, 34; shift of, 36
Organization of Petroleum
    Exporting Countries (OPEC), 72
Overbeek, H., 109
ozone layer, hole in, 42, 60

P2 lodge, 106, 122
Packard, David, 119
passive revolution, 112
peace movement, 140
pessimism, 24, 96
Philippines, 142
van der Pijl, Kees, 23, 24, 86
Pinay Circle, 124
Pinochet, Augusto, 122
political economy, 22; as critical
    theory, 32, 35; classical, 2, 6, 8;
    critical, 31–45, 69; critique of, 7;
    modern, 6; national, 7; nature of,
    1–6, 32
Polanyi, Karl, 3–6, 11, 13, 14, 19–21,
    22, 35, 39, 66–7, 81, 86, 103
political aspect, 2, 5, 8; definition of,
    3; distinct from economic, 6
political science, 32
political society, 85
political correctness, 54
pollution, 41; by rich countries, 42
poor people, disciplining of, 89
Popper, Karl, 122
population, superfluous, 40
post-globalization, 39–41
post-hegemonic world, 17, 36, 43,
    74
post-modernism, 35
post-Westphalian schema, 10, 12, 13,
    17, 21, 36–9
poverty, 74, 134; elimination of,
    142

powerlessness, 138, 143; of the
    powerful, 131; power of, 24, 70,
    96
Prince Rupert, 105
privatization, 39, 78, 83, 118; of
    health care, 90; of security, 89; of
    wealth, 117
production, restructuring of, 75–8
protectionism, 18
public-choice school, 83

quasi-governmental organizations
    (quangos), 82

racism: ethical, 106; in Germany, 54
Reagan, Ronald, 106, 124
realism, 55
reciprocity, 4, 5, 12, 24
Red Army, as tax collectors, 84
redistribution, 4, 5, 12
regionalism, 18; new, 19, 20
regionalization of the world, 18, 19
regions: mega-sized, 75; micro-, 37
Renan, Ernst, 137
rentier, resurgence of, 113, 115
resistance, forms of, 96
restructuring, 75–8
Rhineland model, 94
Rhodes Trust, 107, 121
Rhodes, Cecil, 106
Ricardo, David, 7, 8
right-wing politics, 79, 94, 95
risk, socialization of, 89
Rockefeller, David, 72, 123
Rolland, Romain, 66
Rosenau, James, 17, 22, 24
Roundheads, 102, 103, 104, 110;
    displacement of, 112
Royal Institute of International
    Affairs, 106
Russia, 94, 130

Sakamoto, Yoshikazu, 23, 24, 96
Salinas de Gortari, C., 73
Schumpeter, Joseph, 96
science, globalization of, 131–3
security, privatization of, 89
self, concept of, 140

self-environment orientation, 57, 59, 61

Senghaas, D., 101, 111

shopping malls, fortification of, 89

Shultz, George, 124

Simonsen, Mario, 116

Skocpol, T., 13

Smith, Adam, 7, 44

social conflict, changing nature of, 38

social inequality, 66, 94

social movements, 55, 60, 129–43; new, 36, 94, 140; transnational, 51

social polarization, 36

social science, 68; historical, 6, 14

socialism, 5; breakdown of subsystem, 8

sociology, historical, 13

solidarity, 45, 141

South Africa, 104

South Korea, 95, 117

sovereignty, redefinition of, 84

Star Wars project, 119

starvation, in Third World, 74

state, 8, 37, 69; as historical creation, 34; as main actor, 55; breakdown of economic control, 118; building of, 129; changes in form, 80; changes in system, 9; competition, 81; defined in military terms, 130; entity of, 37; explosion in numbers of, 60; fiscal crisis of, 80, 91; formation of, 7, 107; French, 109; ineffectuality of, 131; internationalization of, 129–31; logic of, 2, 3; perceived as enemy, 36; rolling back of, 82; sovereign, 110, 111, 139; strengthened in US, 108; system, 12

state mode of production, 111

state monopoly tendency, 121

state/society-complexes, 102–13

states, sovereignty of, 12 (decline of, 13)

Strange, Susan, 38, 43, 77

Strauss, Franz-Josef, 124

structural adjustment, 80, 94

structural adjustment programmes (SAPs), 84, 91, 92

structuralism, 9

subgroupism, 60, 61

subnational groupings, 58

supra-intersubjectivity, 21, 24, 43

surveillance, 82, 83, 90, 103; technology of, 87

Swedish model, 88

Taiwan, 95

taxation, 90; collection of, 83; evasion of, 84; increase in, 91; indirect, 84; resistance to, 89

technology, globalization of, 131–3

telecommunications monopolies, 117

Thatcher, Margaret, 44

theory, 48; critical, 32; problem-solving, 31, 35; role of, 31–2; time-bound, 35

Third World, fragmentation of, 72

de Tocqueville, A., 102, 104, 110

Toffler, Alvin, 74

tourism, 50

trade unions, 51

transformation; global, 1; international political economy and, 10–17

transition, 10

transnational entities, 58, 75, 117

The Triad, 18

Trilateral Commission (TC), 86, 123

Tullock, Gordon, 83

turbulence, 1, 10, 12, 22, 23, 60, 95

underdevelopment, 112; development of, 111

unemployment, 16, 54, 78, 82, 88, 90, 96, 131

UNICEF, 92

Union of Soviet Socialist Republics (USSR), 71, 85, 117, 123, 138; arms race with, 119; collapse of, 100, 135

United Kingdom (UK), 4, 7, 37, 67, 70, 81, 82, 122, 130; hegemony of, 11, 14 (decline of, 4)

United Nations (UN): strengthening

of, 131; cutback in development assistance, 41

United States of America (USA), 4, 11, 13, 15, 18, 37, 43, 54, 67, 70, 71, 72, 73, 77, 82, 85, 88, 90, 104, 108, 116, 117, 119, 122, 123, 130, 138; hegemony of, 15, 20; decline of, 4, 16

US Federal Reserve, 119, 123

universalism, 136

Vico, Giambattista, 45

Virginia Company, 104

Volcker, Paul, 119, 123, 124

voting patterns in USA, 88, 89

wage labour, 101

Wallerstein, I., 13, 14

Washington, George, 106

water, access to, 74

Watson, Thomas, 119

wealth, inequalities of, 77

Weber, Max, 34

welfare state, 5, 11, 76; shift from, 81

Westphalian schema, 10, 12, 21, 22

White Anglo-Saxon Protestants, 104

Williamson, David, 125

women, 95; and transformation of public sector, 93; as subsistence farmers, 41; as workers, 76; coalitions in public sector, 93; deteriorating position of, 69; empowerment of, 142; needs of, 92; peasant, 78; poor, 73 (access to credit, 141); Third World, 91, 92; work-load of, 92

women's movement, 93, 140

work, intensification of, 90

workfare, 89

World Bank, 37, 71, 73, 84, 92, 95

World Economic Forum, 86

world order, 129–43; conceptualization of, 67–74; constitution of, 15; meaning of, 65

world-system theories, 9

Yugoslavia, former, 54, 135